SAS/IML™ Guide for Personal Computers, Version 6 Edition

SAS Institute Inc.
Box 8000
Cary, North Carolina 27511-8000

Larry D. Crum and Alice T. Allen edited the *SAS/IML™ User's Guide for Personal Computers, Version 6 Edition*. David D. Baggett and Betty Fried copyedited the text.

The correct bibliographic citation for this manual is as follows: SAS Institute Inc. *SAS/IML™ User's Guide for Personal Computers, Version 6 Edition*. Cary, NC: SAS Institute Inc., 1985. 243 pp.

SAS/IML™ User's Guide, Version 5 Edition

Copyright © 1985 by SAS Institute Inc., Cary, NC, USA.
ISBN 0-917382-96-X

86   4   3   2

Base SAS® software, the foundation of the SAS System, provides data retrieval and management, programming, statistical, and reporting capabilities. Also in the SAS System are SAS/GRAPH®, SAS/FSP®, SAS/ETS®, SAS/IMS-DL/I®, SAS/OR®, SAS/AF®, SAS/REPLAY-CICS®, SAS/DMI®, SAS/QC®, SAS/RTERM®, SAS/IML™, SAS/STAT™, SAS/SHARE™, and SAS/DB2™software. These products and SYSTEM 2000® Data Base Management System, including basic SYSTEM 2000®, QueX™, Multi-User™, Screen Writer™, CREATE™, DISKMGR™ and CICS interface software, are available from SAS Institute Inc., a private company devoted to the support and further development of the software and related services. *SAS Communications®, SAS Training®, SAS Views®,* and SASware Ballot® are published by SAS Institute Inc.

Contents

iv

Illustration

Tables

Tables

Credits

John P. Sall is the development leader for SAS/IML Version 6 and is responsible for designing and documenting the software.

Alan R. Eaton is the SAS/IML Product Manager for Version 5 and Version 6, and he contributed to many parts of SAS/IML Version 6 implementation.

Other major implementation contributors include **Jack J. Rouse**, **G. Kenneth Howell**, **Kathryn Ng**, **Phil Spector**, **Claire S. Cates**, **Leigh A. Ihnen**, **David M. DeLong**, and **Warren S. Sarle**.

Testing contributors include: **Eric Brinsfield**, **Maura Stokes**, and **Glenda Stenbuck**.

Acknowledgments

The GSORTH and ORPOL functions were contributed by **Ronald Helms** of the University of North Carolina at Chapel Hill. The GSORTH function is based on a method described by Golub (1969). The ORPOL function is based on a method described by Emerson (1968).

The OPSCAL function was contributed by **Forrest W. Young** and **Warren F. Kuhfeld** of the University of North Carolina at Chapel Hill. Forrest Young also assisted in developing the example that uses the Multiple Optimal Regression and Alternating Least Squares technique.

Preface

The *SAS/IML User's Guide for Personal Computers, Version 6 Edition* documents SAS/IML software, an interactive matrix language. This manual includes comprehensive descriptions of all SAS/IML commands, functions, and statements, as well as extensive examples of their uses.

If you are a new SAS/IML user, or if you are unfamiliar with SAS procedures operating in an interactive environment, you should first read Part I, "Introduction." This unit includes a general introduction to the language and provides simple introductory sessions. Part II, "Language Guide," describes important components of SAS/IML, and Part III, "Extended Examples," includes many useful examples. Once you are familiar with SAS/IML fundamentals, you can consult Part IV, "SAS/IML Language Reference," for details of each operator, function, and command.

SAS/IML supercedes the MATRIX procedure that was documented in the *SAS User's Guide: Statistics, 1982 Edition*. If you are an experienced user of PROC MATRIX, you may want to read Appendix 1, "SAS/IML Software Compared to PROC MATRIX," for a summary of differences. Also of interest to MATRIX users is Appendix 4, "The MATRIX/IML Translator Procedure."

What is the SAS System?

The SAS System is a software system for data analysis. The goal of SAS Institute is to provide data analysts one system to meet all their computing needs. When your computing needs are met, you are free to concentrate on results rather than on the mechanics of getting them. Instead of learning programming languages, several statistical packages, and utility programs, you only need to learn the SAS System.

To the all-purpose base SAS software, you can add tools for graphics, forecasting, data entry, and interfaces to other data bases to provide one total system. The SAS System runs in batch and interactively under OS, TSO, CMS, VSE, SSX, and ICCF on IBM 370/30xx/43xx and compatible machines; on Digital Equipment Corporation's VAX™8xxx series and 11/7xx series under VMS™ and on MicroVAX II™ under MicroVMS;™ on Data General Corporation's ECLIPSE® MV series under AOS/VS; on Prime Computer, Inc.'s Prime 50 Series under PRIMOS® on the IBM PC AT/370 and XT/370 under VM/PC; and on the IBM PC XT and PC AT under PC DOS.To use any software product in the SAS System, you first need base SAS software. The PL/I Optimizing Transient Library is required for mainframe and VM/PC IBM systems. SYSTEM 2000 DBMS supports IBM 370/30xx/43xx and compatible machines under OS, TSO, CMS, DOS/VS(E), and CICS; the Sperry Series 1100 under OS 1100; and the Control Data 6000 and Cyber series under NOS and NOS/BE. Note: not all products are available for all operating systems.

Base SAS software provides tools for:

- information storage and retrieval
- data modification and programming
- report writing

VAX and VMS are trademarks of Digital Equipment Corp., Maynard, MA, USA.
PRIMOS is the registered trademark of Prime Computer, Inc., Framingham, MA, USA.
ECLIPSE is the registered trademark of Data General Corp., Westboro, MA, USA.

- statistical analysis
- file handling.

Information storage and retrieval   The SAS System reads data values in virtually any form from cards, disk, or tape and then organizes the values into a SAS data set. The data can be combined with other SAS data sets using the file-handling operations described below. The data can be analyzed statistically and can be used to produce reports. SAS data sets are automatically self-documenting since they contain both the data values and their descriptions. The special structure of a SAS data library minimizes maintenance.

Data modification and programming   A complete set of SAS statements and functions is available for modifying data. Some program statements perform standard operations such as creating new variables, accumulating totals, and checking for errors; others are powerful programming tools such as DO/END and IF-THEN/ELSE statements. The data-handling features are so valuable that base SAS software is used by many as a data base management system.

Report writing   Just as base SAS software reads data in almost any form, it can write data in almost any form. In addition to the preformatted reports that SAS procedures produce, SAS software users can design and produce printed reports in any form, including output files on disk.

Statistical analysis   The statistical analysis procedures in the SAS System are among the finest available. They range from simple descriptive statistics to complex multivariate techniques. Their designs are based on our belief that you should never need to tell the SAS System anything it can figure out by itself. Statistical integrity is thus accompanied by ease of use.

File handling   Combining values and observations from several data sets is often necessary for data analysis. SAS software has tools for editing, subsetting, concatenating, merging, and updating data sets. Multiple input files can be processed simultaneously, and several reports can be produced in one pass of the data.

Other SAS System Products

With base SAS software, you can integrate SAS software products to provide one total system. Among other products scheduled to become available on personal computers are:

- SAS/STAT software—a wide range of statistical applications for data analysis and estimation
- SAS/FSP software—interactive, menu-driven facilities for data entry, editing, retrieval of SAS files, letter writing, and spreadsheet analysis
- SAS/GRAPH software—device-intelligent color graphics for business and research applications
- SAS/OR software—decision support tools for operations research and project management
- SAS/AF software—a full-screen, interactive applications facility
- SAS/ETS software—expanded tools for business analysis, forecasting, and financial planning.

SAS Institute Documentation

SAS release?   To find out which release of SAS software you are using, run any SAS job and look at the release number in the notes at the beginning of the SAS log. This user's guide documents Version 6 SAS/IML software.

Other SAS Institute manuals and technical reports   Below is a list of other manuals that document Version 6 SAS System software:

SAS Language Guide for Personal Computers, Version 6 Edition
SAS Procedures Guide for Personal Computers, Version 6 Edition
SAS Introductory Guide for Personal Computers, Version 6 Edition
SAS/STAT Guide for Personal Computers, Version 6 Edition

The SAS Technical Report Series documents work in progress and covers a variety of applications areas. Some of the features described in these reports are still in experimental form and are not yet available as SAS procedures.

Write to SAS Institute for a current publications catalog, which describes the manuals as well as technical reports and lists their prices.

SAS Services to Users

Technical support   SAS Institute supports users through the Technical Support Department. If you have a problem running a SAS job, you should contact your site's SAS Software Consultant. If the problem cannot be resolved locally, your local support personnel should call the Institute's Technical Support Department at (919) 467-8000 on weekdays between 9:00 a.m. and 5:00 p.m. Eastern Standard Time. A brochure describing the services provided by the Technical Support Department is available from SAS Institute.

Training   SAS Institute sponsors a comprehensive training program, including programs of study for novice data processors, statisticians, applications programmers, systems programmers, and local support personnel. *SAS Training*, a semi-annual training publication, describes the total training program and each course currently being offered by SAS Institute.

News magazine   *SAS Communications* is the quarterly news magazine of SAS Institute. Each issue contains ideas for more effective use of the SAS System, information about research and development underway at SAS Institute, the current training schedule, new publications, and news of the SAS Users Group International (SUGI).

To receive a copy of *SAS Communications* regularly, send your name and complete address to:

SAS Institute Mailing List
SAS Institute Inc.
Box 8000
Cary, NC 27511-8000

SUGI

The SAS Users Group International (SUGI) is a nonprofit association of professionals who are interested in how others are using the SAS System. Although SAS Institute provides administrative support, SUGI is independent from the Institute. Membership is open to all users at SAS sites, and there is no membership fee.

Annual conferences are structured to allow many avenues of discussion. Users present invited and contributed papers on various topics, for example:

- computer performance evaluation and systems software
- econometrics and time series
- graphics
- information systems
- interactive techniques

- statistics
- tutorials in SAS System software.

Proceedings of the annual conferences are distributed free to SUGI registrants. Extra copies may be purchased from SAS Institute.

SASware Ballot   SAS users provide valuable input toward the direction of future SAS development by ranking their priorities on the annual SASware Ballot. The top vote-getters are announced at the SUGI conference. Complete results of the SASware Ballot are also printed in the *SUGI Proceedings*.

Supplemental library   Under many operating systems (not yet including PC DOS), SAS users have written their own SAS procedures for a wide variety of specialized applications. SAS Institute will notify your SAS Software Consultant when this facility is available for microcomputers.

Licensing the SAS System

The SAS System is licensed to customers in the Western Hemisphere from the Institute's headquarters in Cary, NC. To serve the needs of our international customers, the Institute maintains subsidiaries in the United Kingdom, New Zealand, Australia, Singapore, Germany, and France. In addition, agents in other countries are licensed distributors for the SAS System. For a complete list of offices, write or call:

SAS Institute Inc.
SAS Circle
Box 8000
Cary, NC 27511-8000
(919) 467-8000

PART I: INTRODUCTION

Introduction to SAS/IML™ Software

Introductory Demonstration Session

Introduction to SAS/IML™ for
Lists and Tables

Introduction to SAS/IML™ for
Mathematics and Statistics

Introduction to SAS/IML™ for
Data Processing

PART I.
INTRODUCTION

## Chapter 1

Introduction to SAS/IML™ Software

SAS/IML software consists of the SAS IML procedure that implements a programming language called the IML language (Interactive Matrix Language).

IML is a multi-level interactive programming language. You can use IML commands to tune in to the finest detail or reach out to large operations processing thousands of values. You can execute statements immediately or layer statements into modules to store and execute later. IML variables can hold anything from a single character to thousands of elements. You can store everything into a file and load it back at a later time.

IML is flexible yet powerful. Many languages are very flexible, but low-level; that is, you must program every detail. Other languages are high-level; that is, you specify what to do rather than how to do it, but you are limited to operations that are already integrated into the system. IML addresses both needs: when you want to do something fairly common, IML has high-level operations to do them concisely, and when you want to customize something, you can program it your way with the IML programming language.

The multi-level capabilities of IML can be illustrated by several examples. Consider the statement

```
X=X+1;
```

which you could use in IML to add 1 to a single value, X, or to a matrix **X** of thousands of elements. In conventional programming languages, you would need looping specifications for the matrix addition.

To retrieve a phone number from a record, you can enter an IML statement similar to those in many programming languages:

```
READ var{phone};
```

To go through all the data to get phone numbers for all individuals whose last name begins with "Smith" is almost as easy:

```
READ all var{phone} where(lastname=:"Smith");
```

instead of writing loops and testing in other languages. The result is a matrix **PHONE** of phone numbers.

There is a lot of literature concerning fourth-generation languages, applications-oriented languages, and non-procedural languages. Despite their appearance, these languages are, in fact, programming languages. Instead of using statements for writing programs, these languages use commands. IML has high-level commands, which you are allowed to program in any way you like as well as mix with customized, low-level instructions.

IML is interactive.   You can execute a command as soon as you enter it, or you can collect commands for later execution. You can also write statements with a text-editor to bring them into an IML session. While many systems depend on you to babysit a session to answer questions, IML only lets you give solid commands, which it then performs without intervention. However, if you want to intervene, you can instruct IML to pause, and you can enter new commands, and resume execution later. You can even be paused in dozens of modules simultaneously, and resume them as needed.

IML has a totally open architecture.   You can use each IML command in any context; IML has no modes to restrict access to certain commands. Except for module definition statements, all commands have uniform status.

- All commands are executable.
- All commands can be either executed immediately or stored in modules.
- All commands can be executed conditionally.
- All commands can be programmed into loops.

IML has a dynamic nature.   A variable can change its dimension and type at any time. Many files can be opened. Many libraries can be accessed. Options can be reset at any time. Modules can be replaced.

IML is a programming language.   IML is a complete language with features for arithmetic and character expressions, data input and output, control of execution, and program modularization.

IML data elements are matrices.   Most programming languages deal with single data elements; the fundamental data element in IML is a matrix, a two-dimensional (row-by-column) array of numeric (double-precision, real, floating-point) values.

IML expressions use operators that apply to entire matrices.   For example, the expression A+B in IML adds the elements of the two matrices A and B. The expression A*B performs a matrix multiplication, while A#B does elementwise multiplication of the values in A and B.

IML incorporates a powerful vocabulary of operators.   Matrix operations that require calls to math-library subroutines in other languages are built into IML. Most programming languages have six to ten operators and a small function library. IML offers several dozen operators, functions, and call routines.

IML avoids housekeeping work typical in other programming languages.   In many languages you must explicitly declare, dimension, or allocate storage for a data item, and you cannot change its attributes once it is declared. In contrast, IML does all the housekeeping automatically. The attributes of a matrix are determined when the matrix is given a value. The procedure automatically finds space as needed for a matrix of any size. A matrix can change in size and attributes at any time.

IML operations allow more direct programming.   IML eliminates most iterative specifications, calls to math subroutines, declarations, and allocations. For example, finding the sum of all positive elements of a matrix **X** requires one line in IML:

```
S = SUM( X # (X>0));
```

The expression involves the sum of an elementwise product of two items. The first item is the matrix **X**; the second item is an indicator matrix showing the positive values of **X**. Once you have learned the matrix notation, this operation is clearer and more direct than an iterative specification that would be necessary in other programming languages such as PL/I:

```
SUM=0;
DO I=1 TO N;
   DO J=1 TO M;
      IF X(I,J)>0 THEN SUM=SUM+X(I,J);
      END;
   END;
```

IML notation is compact.   Since IML operations deal with arrays of numbers and the most commonly used mathematical and matrix operations are built directly into the language, programs that take hundreds of lines of code in other languages may take only a few lines in IML.

IML allows you to think directly in matrix algebra terms.   If you are a statistician, you already know the formulas for many statistical methods. But in most languages, it is no easy job to transcribe these formulas into a program. In IML, you can transcribe almost directly from matrix algebra notation into IML program statements. For example, the formula for the least-squares estimates of parameters in a linear model in matrix notation is written:

$$\mathbf{b} = (\mathbf{X'X})^{-1}\mathbf{X'y}.$$

It can be written in IML as:

```
B=INV(X`*X)*X`*Y;
```

IML is an alternative to APL.   APL is another language that deals with matrices of values. Unlike IML, however, APL works with a specialized character set that takes time to learn and is available only on special terminals. IML can be learned more quickly than APL since it builds on traditional and more familiar notation.

IML has a rich set of control statements.   IML allows you to program with control statements including LINK, GOTO, IF-THEN/ELSE, DO/END, iterative DO, and STOP.

IML allows you to stay close to the original problem.   Every time you make housekeeping specifications in another programming language, you are distracted from the original problem. Since IML code is easier and clearer than most programming languages, you stay closer to the heart of the problem and have opportunities for greater insights. Shorter IML programs allow you a better overall perspective of the work instead of an endless stream of detail.

IML does data processing.   You can read entire SAS data sets or selected observations from SAS data sets into IML variables. A single statement can create multiple vectors, one for each variable on the data set, or a matrix that contains a column for each data set variable. You can also create new SAS data sets and append observations to existing SAS data sets using IML statements.

Cautions when using IML:

- IML does not recognize missing values except for certain operations.
- IML is inefficient for certain highly iterative applications. These problems, especially those with subscripting, require overhead for interpretive execution and housekeeping activities. Fortunately, however, highly iterative applications can usually be recoded into matrix operations.

## Chapter 2

Introductory Demonstration Session

Getting Started

If you are new to IML, follow this introductory session to see how easy IML is to use. To begin, get into the SAS System and enter

```
> proc iml;
```

IML responds with the message

```
IML ready
```

The statements you enter are shown in this book after the > character. PROC IML responds immediately to each statement you submit.

First, tell IML to print all results automatically so you do not have to ask for results each time:

```
> reset print;
```

Creating Matrices

Entering data in a matrix   The IML language handles data in a two-dimensional array called a *matrix*. Try putting some data into a matrix by entering:

```
> a=2;
```

IML responds by printing out the value for the new matrix **A**.

```
          A          1 rows    1 columns
                         2
```

Next, set up another matrix, this time with several values:

```
> b={1 2 3 4};
```

The braces { } enclose multiple values into a matrix. IML responds with the value
for the new matrix **B**:

```
          B          1 rows    4 columns
               1         2         3         4
```

If you want to create a matrix with several rows, separate the rows with commas

```
> c={0 1 0 0, 2 1 0 0, 0 1 0 4};
```

IML responds with

```
          C          3 rows    4 columns
              0         1         0         0
              2         1         0         0
              0         1         0         4
```

C now has 12 values arranged in 3 rows and 4 columns.

Listing matrices and attributes   **A**, **B**, and **C**, the matrices you have defined so
far, retain their values until you change them or exit IML. If you forget which
matrices you defined, you can show their names and attributes with

```
> show names;
```

which produces this list:

```
          A          1 rows    1 cols  num     8
          B          1 rows    4 cols  num     8
          C          3 rows    4 cols  num     8
              Number of matrices 3
```

Displaying matrix values   To go back and look at the values in a matrix, use the
command

```
> print b;
```

which gives these results:

```
B
1            2           3           4
```

Other Matrix Operations

Using IML expressions   You have seen the simplest way to create a new matrix and give it values. You can also give values to a matrix by using the name of an existing matrix as a variable in an IML assignment statement.

Suppose that you want to create **D** as **A** plus 12:

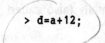

```
> d=a+12;
```

Using **A**'s previous value, **D** becomes:

```
D             1 rows    1 columns
14
```

If you add 12 to **B**,

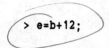

```
> e=b+12;
```

you get these results:

```
E             1 rows    4 columns
13            14           15          16
```

This is the way IML allows you to add a value to each element of a matrix. You can also subtract, multiply, and divide.

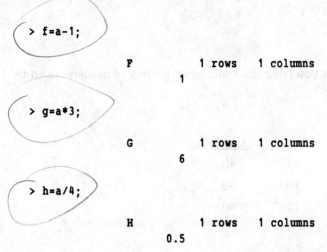

```
> f=a-1;
```

```
F             1 rows    1 columns
1
```

```
> g=a*3;
```

```
G             1 rows    1 columns
6
```

```
> h=a/4;
```

```
H             1 rows    1 columns
0.5
```

Changing values in a matrix   Suppose that you want to assign a different value to **A**:

```
> a={2,5};
```

```
A                2 rows    1 columns
                 2
                 5
```

You can give new values to a matrix at any time, even values that change the dimension of the matrix.

Joining matrices   The || operator joins two matrices horizontally (also called *concatenate*) to form a larger matrix.

```
> a=a||a;
```

In this case, **A** is horizontally joined to itself:

```
A                2 rows    2 columns
                 2          2
                 5          5
```

If you want to join matrices vertically, use the // operator

```
> b=a//{0 1};
```

which produces these results:

```
B                3 rows    2 columns
                 2          2
                 5          5
                 0          1
```

Multiplying   Suppose that you have the number of gallons of gasoline used by two cars for three months:

Month	Car A	Car B
Jan	23	40
Feb	10	30
Mar	15	40

These data form a 3-row by 2-column matrix

```
> gas=(23 40,
>      10 30,
>      15 40);
```

printed by IML as:

```
GAS       3 rows    2 columns
    23        40
    10        30
    15        40
```

If gasoline averages $1.35 per gallon, you can calculate the monthly cost:

```
> cost=gas*1.35;
```

with these results:

```
COST      3 rows    2 columns
   31.05        54
   13.5       40.5
   20.25        54
```

Note that IML performed six multiplications as a result of one simple expression.

Suppose that car A uses unleaded gasoline, car B uses leaded, and gasoline costs vary from month-to-month.

Month	Car A	Car B
Jan	1.35	1.25
Feb	1.40	1.35
Mar	1.30	1.27

Use this IML statement

```
> price=(1.35 1.25, 1.40 1.35, 1.30 1.27);
```

to put the data into matrix form:

```
PRICE     3 rows    2 columns
   1.35      1.25
   1.4       1.35
   1.3       1.27
```

Now try to compute new costs:

```
> cost=price*gas;
```

IML tells you that your specification was wrong:

```
Error: (EXECUTION)  Matrices do not conform to the operation
```

In this IML statement you want to multiply corresponding elements of the two matrices; however, in IML and matrix algebra the matrix multiplication operator has a different meaning. To multiply corresponding matrix elements, use the elementwise multiply operator # shown below:

```
> cost=price#gas;
```

with these results:

```
        COST        3 rows   2 columns
              31.05          50
              14           40.5
              19.5         50.8
```

Summing   Use the SUM function to find the total cost of gas for both cars

```
> s=sum(cost);
```

which produces:

```
        S           1 rows   1 columns
            205.85
```

Leaving IML

The way to exit IML is

```
> quit;
```

The procedure responds:

```
Exiting IML.

NOTE : The PROCEDURE IML used  1: 6:57 seconds.
```

## Chapter 3

Introduction to SAS/IML™ for Lists and Tables

This chapter illustrates operations on IML lists and tables (mathematicians refer to these as vectors and matrices).

If you are not already in the IML procedure, enter

```
> proc iml;
```

If you are still in IML from the demonstration session in the last section, use the command below to reset the PRINT option.

```
> reset noprint;
```

(You want to experiment with some of PRINT's features and do not want the results printed automatically.)

Suppose you need 1 pound of carrots, 3 cucumbers, 2 heads of lettuce, and 6 potatoes. Instead of writing this grocery list on the back of an envelope, you enter each item into an IML variable.

```
> carrots=1;
> cukes=3;
> lettuce=2;
> potatoes=6;
> print carrots cukes lettuce potatoes;
```

```
        CARROTS      CUKES   LETTUCE  POTATOES
              1          3         2         6
```

Now you have a list, but it is not organized the way you want it—to print it, you do not want to be required to type in the name of each variable. Try putting all the items in one variable as shown below:

```
> quant={1,3,2,6};
> print quant;
```

```
QUANT
  1
  3
  2
  6
```

The braces { } are the punctuation marks for enclosing this list of numbers. IML also allows you to use names, so enter:

```
> item={carrots,cukes,lettuce,potatoes};
```

This PRINT command can print the two lists side-by-side:

```
> print item quant;
```

```
ITEM        QUANT
CARROTS       1
CUKES         3
LETTUCE       2
POTATOES      6
```

or you can list quantities with items as row names:

```
> print quant[rowname=item];
```

```
            QUANT
CARROTS       1
CUKES         3
LETTUCE       2
POTATOES      6
```

Suppose relatives visit, and you need to double the quantities:

```
> quant2=quant*2;
> print quant2[rowname=item];
```

```
            QUANT2
CARROTS        2
CUKES          6
LETTUCE        4
POTATOES      12
```

The [ ] notation (called *subscripting*) is a way of referring to specific elements of a list. Suppose that you only need to increase your original carrot order by 1:

```
> quant[1]=quant[1]+1;
> print quant[rowname=item];
```

```
                    QUANT
           CARROTS     2
           CUKES       3
           LETTUCE     2
           POTATOES    6
```

If you want to find the location of an element, use the LOC function:

```
> i=loc(item={lettuce});
> print i;
```

```
               I
               3
```

The LOC function returns the position where the ITEM list has the value
LETTUCE. You are now ready to go to the nearest grocery store and scout out
the prices.

```
> price={1.23, .33, 1.45, .12};
> print item quant price;
```

```
          ITEM      QUANT     PRICE
          CARROTS     2       1.23
          CUKES       3       0.33
          LETTUCE     3       1.45
          POTATOES    6       0.12
```

You need the costs—the prices multiplied by the quantities:

```
> cost=price#quant;
> print item quant price cost;
```

```
          ITEM      QUANT    PRICE    COST
          CARROTS     2      1.23     2.46
          CUKES       3      0.33     0.99
          LETTUCE     3      1.45     4.35
          POTATOES    6      0.12     0.72
```

The # is a special multiplication operator to multiply corresponding lists of values, element by element; to multiply a list by a single element, use either * or
#. (In other programming languages you must use loops to do operations on lists
of values.)

What is the total cost?

```
> total=sum(cost);
> print total;
```

```
          TOTAL
          8.52
```

The SUM function adds up all the elements of the list. Another way to do this is

```
> total=cost[+];
```

which uses the subscript operator to add the elements.

Those prices were at the Saleway store. You also check prices at several other stores: Kruger, A&G, Foodcity, and Bigmart.

```
> saleway =price;
> kruger  ={ 1.21, .35, 1.41, .19};
> ag      ={ 1.18, .35, 1.42, .11};
> foodcity={ 1.43, .39, 1.52, .46};
> bigmart ={ .99, .29, .99, .21};
> print item saleway kruger ag foodcity bigmart;
```

ITEM	SALEWAY	KRUGER	AG	FOODCITY	BIGMART
CARROTS	1.23	1.21	1.18	1.43	0.99
CUKES	0.33	0.35	0.35	0.39	0.29
LETTUCE	1.45	1.41	1.42	1.52	0.99
POTATOES	0.12	0.19	0.11	0.46	0.21

Now, to decide where to shop, compute costs and totals for each store:

```
> salecost =  saleway # quant;
> krugcost =   kruger # quant;
> agcost   =       ag # quant;
> foodcost = foodcity # quant;
> bigcost  =  bigmart # quant;
> saletot  = sum(salecost);
> krugtot  = sum(krugcost);
> agtot    = sum(agcost);
> foodtot  = sum(foodcost);
> bigtot   = sum(bigcost);
> print item salecost krugcost agcost foodcost bigcost,
>        " TOTAL " saletot krugtot agtot foodtot bigtot;
```

ITEM	SALECOST	KRUGCOST	AGCOST	FOODCOST	BIGCOST
CARROTS	2.46	2.42	2.36	2.86	1.98
CUKES	0.99	1.05	1.05	1.17	0.87
LETTUCE	4.35	4.23	4.26	4.56	2.97
POTATOES	0.72	1.14	0.66	2.76	1.26

	SALETOT	KRUGTOT	AGTOT	FOODTOT	BIGTOT
TOTAL	8.52	8.84	8.33	11.35	7.08

You decide to shop at Bigmart since it has the lowest total cost of 7.08.

The last group of calculations would have been much easier if you had organized your data on a higher level. Nevertheless, using lists made the operations more powerful by distributing operations across a dimension. Similarly, you can make your operations still more powerful by using tables to distribute operations across two dimensions.

```
> price=saleway||kruger||ag||foodcity||bigmart;
> print price;
```

```
        PRICE
        1.23      1.21      1.18      1.43      0.99
        0.33      0.35      0.35      0.39      0.29
        1.45      1.41      1.42      1.52      0.99
        0.12      0.19      0.11      0.46      0.21
```

You have created a PRICE table with four rows representing the food items and five columns representing the stores. You used the || operator to join the lists horizontally, but you could have entered all the data into a table like this:

```
> price = {1.23    1.21    1.18    1.43    0.99,
>          0.33    0.35    0.35    0.39    0.29,
>          1.45    1.41    1.42    1.52    0.99,
>          0.12    0.19    0.11    0.46    0.21};
```

(A comma separates one row from the next.) Now you border the table with ITEM and a list of the store names, using the abbreviations for ROWNAME and COLNAME in the PRINT command.

```
> stores={saleway kruger ag foodcity bigmart};
> print price[r=item c=stores];
```

PRICE	SALEWAY	KRUGER	AG	FOODCITY	BIGMART
CARROTS	1.23	1.21	1.18	1.43	0.99
CUKES	0.33	0.35	0.35	0.39	0.29
LETTUCE	1.45	1.41	1.42	1.52	0.99
POTATOES	0.12	0.19	0.11	0.46	0.21

What are the costs? Again use the # multiplication operator, this time to multiply the columns of the table by the column of quantities desired:

```
> cost=price#quant;
> print cost[r=item c=stores];
```

COST	SALEWAY	KRUGER	AG	FOODCITY	BIGMART
CARROTS	2.46	2.42	2.36	2.86	1.98
CUKES	0.99	1.05	1.05	1.17	0.87
LETTUCE	4.35	4.23	4.26	4.56	2.97
POTATOES	0.72	1.14	0.66	2.76	1.26

For each store (column), what are the cost totals across the items (rows)? Use the + operator across the row subscript:

```
> total=cost[+,];
> print total[colname=stores];
```

```
TOTAL  SALEWAY   KRUGER      AG FOODCITY BIGMART
        8.52     8.84     8.33    11.35     7.08
```

Compare these calculations with the previous ones to notice the power of table arithmetic.

You can even use subscript operators to look across rows or columns to find minimum or maximum values. For each item (row), what is the store (column) with the lowest cost? Use the column subscript index with the minimum operator on COST to choose the STORES element. (This is a bit of fancy, but concise, code to find out that Bigmart has the cheapest cost for everything except potatoes.)

```
> least=stores[cost[,>:<]] ;
> print least[r=item];
```

```
        LEAST

                CARROTS  BIGMART
                CUKES    BIGMART
                LETTUCE  BIGMART
                POTATOES AG
```

You computed total cost per store by multiplying a table by a list and using a summation subscript. Another approach using the transpose and cross-product operators will prove to have advantages later.

The transpose operator, written as a backquote mark (`) following the variable, interchanges the rows and columns of a table. You need to transpose the price table:

```
> tprice=price ` ;
> print price[rowname=item   colname=stores],
>        tprice [rowname=stores colname=item];
```

```
PRICE     SALEWAY    KRUGER       AG FOODCITY  BIGMART
CARROTS      1.23      1.21     1.18     1.43     0.99
CUKES        0.33      0.35     0.35     0.39     0.29
LETTUCE      1.45      1.41     1.42     1.52     0.99
POTATOES     0.12      0.19     0.11     0.46     0.21
```

```
TPRICE    CARROTS    CUKES  LETTUCE POTATOES
SALEWAY      1.23      0.33     1.45     0.12
KRUGER       1.21      0.35     1.41     0.19
AG           1.18      0.35     1.42     0.11
FOODCITY     1.43      0.39     1.52     0.46
BIGMART      0.99      0.29     0.99     0.21
```

The numbers in PRICE and TPRICE are the same, but the new TPRICE table is switched around.

The crossproduct operator (*), when its operands are both lists or tables, forms the sums of products of the rows in the first table by the columns in the second table.

```
> cost=tprice*quant;
> print cost[rowname=stores];
```

```
COST
SALEWAY      8.52
KRUGER       8.84
AG           8.33
FOODCITY    11.35
BIGMART      7.08
```

The SALEWAY total is formed by the multiplications and additions of the following TPRICE and QUANT elements:

$$
\begin{aligned}
&1.23 \ * \ 2. \\
+\ &.33 \ * \ 3. \\
+\ &1.45 \ * \ 3. \\
+\ &.12 \ * \ 6. \ = 8.52
\end{aligned}
$$

The result is the same as before, except that the result is transposed. You can use this kind of multiplication whenever <u>the rows of the first operand correspond to columns in the second operand.</u>

The power of cross-multiplication is more evident when both operands are full tables. Consider making grocery lists for six months arranged in a table called QUANT6:

```
> quant6 = {2 2 2 2 1 2,
>           3 4 3 6 3 4,
>           3 3 3 5 3 4,
>           6 5 7 2 7 8};
> months={jan feb mar apr may jun};
> print quant6[rowname=item colname=months];
```

QUANT6	JAN	FEB	MAR	APR	MAY	JUN
CARROTS	2	2	2	2	1	2
CUKES	3	4	3	6	3	4
LETTUCE	3	3	3	5	3	4
POTATOES	6	5	7	2	7	8

Now it is easy to make a table of total costs for store by month: the same calculations are applied to more data:

```
> cost=price ` *quant6;
> print cost[rowname=stores colname=months];
```

COST	JAN	FEB	MAR	APR	MAY	JUN
SALEWAY	8.52	8.73	8.64	11.93	7.41	10.54
KRUGER	8.84	9.	9.03	11.95	7.82	10.98
AG	8.33	8.57	8.44	11.78	7.26	10.32
FOODCITY	11.35	11.28	11.81	13.72	10.38	14.18
BIGMART	7.08	7.16	7.29	9.09	6.3	8.78

The first column of this result is the same as the costs calculated earlier. Now you have the total cost for each month for each store.

Note to mathematicians: the * operator, called *matrix multiplication*, is one of many powerful matrix operators for dealing with systems of linear equations. In our case, the linear equations were for multiplying a series of prices by a series of quantities. IML is very adept at performing such operations.

## Chapter 4

Introduction to SAS/IML™ for Mathematics and Statistics

SAS/IML software is an interactive matrix programming language that features operations on entire matrices of values. The language is patterned directly after matrix algebra notation. For example, the least-squares formula familiar to statisticians

$$B = (X'X)^{-1}X'Y$$

can be easily translated into the IML assignment statement

```
B=INV(X`*X)*X`*Y;
```

If a statistical method has not been implemented directly in a SAS procedure, you may be able to program it using IML. Because the operations in IML deal with arrays of numbers rather than with one number at a time, and the most commonly used mathematical and matrix operations are built directly into the language, programs that take hundreds of lines of code in other languages often take only a few lines in IML. Since IML is built around traditional matrix algebra notation, it is often possible to transcribe statistical methods from matrix algebraic expressions in texts into executable IML statements.

For example, consider the problem of solving these two simultaneous equations:

$$2X_1 + 3X_2 = 5$$
$$X_1 - 4X_2 = -3$$

These equations may be written in matrix form

$$\begin{array}{cccc} 2 & 3 & X_1 & = & 5 \\ 1 & -4 & X_2 & = & -3 \end{array}$$

which can be expressed symbolically as

$$A\,x = c \ .$$

A is nonsingular, and the solution is

$$x = A^{-1}c \ .$$

To use IML to solve the problem, enter the PROC IML statement to get into the procedure:

```
> proc iml;
```

After IML responds with a ready message

```
IML ready
```

enter

```
> reset print;
```

to have IML print your results automatically.
Then you set up the matrices **A** and **C**:

```
> a={2  3,
>     1 -4};
```

```
A          2 rows   2 columns
        2           3
        1          -4
```

```
> c={5,-3};
```

```
C          2 rows   1 columns
        5
       -3
```

After you enter each statement, IML executes it and prints the results.
You now want to write the solution equation

$$x = A^{-1}c$$

as a matrix statement:

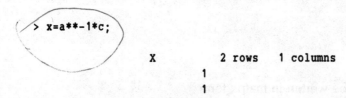

```
> x=a**-1*c;
```

```
X          2 rows   1 columns
        1
        1
```

(Two asterisks denote a power, and one asterisk denotes multiplication as in a SAS program statement.)
After IML executes the statement, the first row of matrix **X** consists of the X_1 value for which you are solving; the second row contains the X_2 value. (Both values happen to be 1.)
A more efficient method for solving this set of equations is the SOLVE function:

```
X=SOLVE(A,C);
```

If **A** is singular, or even if **A** is not square, then you may want to solve the problem with the more general (g-4) generalized inverse operation implemented as the GINV function in IML:

```
X=GINV(A)*C;
```

The GINV function produces a minimum norm result that is a least-squares fit of the linear model. The method is familiar to statisticians if different letters are used. To statisticians, a linear model is usually written

$$y = X b + e$$

where **y** is the vector to fit, **X** is the design matrix, and **b** is to be solved to minimize the sum of squares of **e**, the error or residual. Suppose that your data are

```
> x={1 1 1 ,
>    1 2 4 ,
>    1 3 9 ,
>    1 4 16,
>    1 5 25};
```

	X	5 rows	3 columns
	1	1	1
	1	2	4
	1	3	9
	1	4	16
	1	5	25

```
> y={1,5,9,23,36};
```

	Y	5 rows	1 columns
		1	
		5	
		9	
		23	
		36	

Then the least-squares estimate of **b** can be formed by

```
B=GINV(X)*Y;
```

but you use the more traditional formula:

```
> b=inv(x`*x)*x`*y;
```

	B	3 rows	1 columns
		2.4	
		-3.2	
		2	

You now assume that **X** is full-rank. The predicted values are simply the **X** matrix multiplied into the parameter estimates, and the residuals are the difference between actual and predicted **Y**:

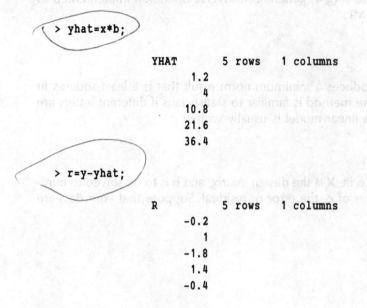

```
> yhat=x*b;
```

```
          YHAT      5 rows    1 columns
                     1.2
                       4
                    10.8
                    21.6
                    36.4
```

```
> r=y-yhat;
```

```
          R         5 rows    1 columns
                    -0.2
                       1
                    -1.8
                     1.4
                    -0.4
```

To measure the fit, calculate the sum of squared errors and mean squared error:

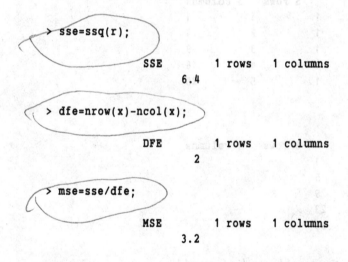

```
> sse=ssq(r);
```

```
          SSE       1 rows    1 columns
                     6.4
```

```
> dfe=nrow(x)-ncol(x);
```

```
          DFE       1 rows    1 columns
                       2
```

```
> mse=sse/dfe;
```

```
          MSE       1 rows    1 columns
                     3.2
```

Note that each calculation has required one simple line of code, whether the problem was very small like the one above or involved larger matrices.

You now want to solve the problem repeatedly without reentering the code. To do this, form a module called REG:

```
>
> /*---module to perform regression, given x and y---*/
> start reg;
>    xpxi=inv(x`*x);
>    beta=xpxi*(x`*y);            /* parameter estimates */
>    yhat=x*beta;                 /* predicted values    */
>    resid=y-yhat;                /* residuals           */
```

```
>     sse=ssq(resid);                  /* sum-of-squared errors */
>     n=nrow(x);                       /* number of observations */
>     dfe=n-ncol(x);                   /* degrees-of-freedom error */
>     mse=sse/dfe;                     /* mean-squared error    */
>     cssy=ssq(y-y[+]/n);              /* SS for y corrected for mean*/
>     rsquare=(cssy-sse)/cssy;         /* measure of fit        */
>     print,"Regression Results" , , sse dfe mse rsquare;
>     stdb=sqrt(vecdiag(xpxi)*mse);    /* standard errors of estimates */
>     t=beta/stdb;                     /* Student's t test: parameters=zero */
>     prob=1-probf(t#t,1,dfe);         /* significance probability */
>     print,"Parameter Estimates" , , beta stdb t prob;
>     print,y yhat resid;
> finish;
>
> reset noprint;
> run reg;
```

```
                       Regression Results

                 SSE      DFE      MSE   RSQUARE
                 6.4        2      3.2 .99235182


                      Parameter Estimates

          BETA      STDB        T       PROB
           2.4 3.8366652 .62554324 .59548008
          -3.2  2.923794 -1.094468 0.387969
             2 .47809144 4.1833001 .05266907


             Y       YHAT      RESID
             1       1.2       -0.2
             5         4          1
             9      10.8       -1.8
            23      21.6        1.4
            36      36.4       -0.4
```

You still have all the matrices ready if you want to continue calculations. Suppose that you want to correlate the estimates. First, calculate the covariance estimate of the estimates; then find and apply values that scale the covariance into a correlation matrix with values of 1 on the diagonals.

```
> reset print;
> covb=xpxi*mse;

              COVB       3 rows   3 columns
              14.72      -10.56        1.6
             -10.56   8.5485714  -1.371429
                1.6   -1.371429 .22857143


> s=1/sqrt(vecdiag(covb));
```

```
                      S           3 rows    1 columns
                        .26064302
                        .34202136
                       2.0916501

> corrb=diag(s)*covb*diag(s);

                   CORRB        3 rows    3 columns
                            1  -.9413763  .87227838
                    -.9413763          1  -.9811049
                    .87227838  -.9811049          1
```

Your module remains available to do a regression on other data—in this case, an orthogonalized version of the last polynomial example. You expect the statistics of fit to be the same and the estimates to be more stable and uncorrelated.

```
> x1=x[,2];

                   X1           5 rows    1 columns
                              1
                              2
                              3
                              4
                              5

> x=orpol(x1,2);

                   X            5 rows    3 columns
                   0.4472136  -.6324555  .53452248
                   0.4472136  -.3162278  -.2672612
                   0.4472136          0  -.5345225
                   0.4472136  .31622777  -.2672612
                   0.4472136  .63245553  .53452248


> reset noprint;
> run reg;

                        Regression Results

            SSE        DFE         MSE       RSQUARE
            6.4          2         3.2     .99235182

                        Parameter Estimates

           BETA        STDB          T         PROB
      33.093806   1.7888544        18.5   0.0029091
      27.828043   1.7888544   15.556349   .00410679
      7.4833148   1.7888544   4.1833001   .05266907
```

```
     Y       YHAT      RESID
     1        1.2       -0.2
     5         4          1
     9       10.8       -1.8
    23       21.6        1.4
    36       36.4       -0.4
```

```
> reset print;
> covb=xpxi*mse;
```

```
        COVB        3 rows    3 columns
             3.2 -7.11E-16 1.243E-15
       -7.11E-16       3.2 5.507E-15
       1.243E-15 5.507E-15       3.2
```

```
> s=1/sqrt(vecdiag(covb));
```

```
        S           3 rows    1 columns
        .55901699
        .55901699
        .55901699
```

```
> corrb=diag(s)*covb*diag(s);
```

```
        CORRB       3 rows    3 columns
               1 -2.22E-16 3.886E-16
       -2.22E-16         1 1.721E-15
       3.886E-16 1.721E-15         1
```

Note that the values on the off-diagonal are printed in scientific notation; the values are close to zero but not exactly zero because of the imprecision of floating point arithmetic.

## Chapter 5

Introduction to SAS/IML™ for Data Processing

Creating a SAS Data Set from IML
Browsing and Listing Data Set Values
Indexing the Data Set

This chapter introduces the data processing features in IML. These features access SAS data sets in many ways: reading, listing, summarizing, searching, modifying, creating, deleting, appending, renaming, sorting, and more. You can have many SAS data sets open simultaneously. You can read one, many, or all records into memory either sequentially, directly by record number, or according to conditions in a WHERE clause. You can index the data sets so that retrievals by value are very fast. You can open and close data sets anytime during the session. You can combine data processing features with file access features and display windows to build simple or complex information systems.

The data processing functions are performed with straightforward, consistent, and powerful commands. For example, the LIST command is very easy to learn, and yet simple variations on this single command can handle the following: list the next record, list a specified record, list any number of specified records, list the whole file, list records satisfying one or more conditions, list specified variables or all variables. Now if you want to read the values into memory, use the READ command instead of LIST with the same operands and features as LIST. As with all IML statements, you can execute these commands interactively or from programs, either iteratively or conditionally. Furthermore, operands can be specified indirectly so that you can dynamically program which records, variables, and conditional values you want.

Creating a SAS Data Set from IML

You can use IML commands to create SAS data sets without leaving the procedure. Suppose you want to create a SAS data set named CLASS containing the variables NAME, SEX, AGE, HEIGHT, and WEIGHT. The > character indicates your input lines; the other lines are responses from IML.
Enter the procedure:

```
> libname user '.';
> proc iml;
```

IML responds with:

```
IML ready
```

You want your results printed automatically in this section so enter

```
> reset print;
```

Your data values, shown below, are in a simple text file named CLASS.DAT:

```
JOYCE    F  11  51.3   50.5
THOMAS   M  11  57.5   85.0
JAMES    M  12  57.3   83.0
JANE     F  12  59.8   84.5
JOHN     M  12  59.0   99.5
LOUISE   F  12  56.3   77.0
ROBERT   M  12  64.8  128.0
ALICE    F  13  56.5   84.0
BARBARA  F  13  65.3   98.0
JEFFREY  M  13  62.5   84.0
CAROL    F  14  62.8  102.5
HENRY    M  14  63.5  102.5
ALFRED   M  14  69.0  112.5
JUDY     F  14  64.3   90.0
JANET    F  15  62.5  112.5
MARY     F  15  66.5  112.0
RONALD   M  15  67.0  133.0
WILLIAM  M  15  66.5  112.0
PHILIP   M  16  72.0  150.0
```

In your first IML command you assign values to NAME and SEX to set the lengths and the type attribute to character; the other variables assume the default numeric type:

```
> name="12345678";
```

```
            NAME        1 rows   1 columns
            12345678
```

```
> sex="m";
```

```
            SEX         1 rows   1 columns
            m
```

You set attributes first since IML must have type and length information for each variable at the time the CREATE command executes to open a new SAS data set:

```
> create class var{name sex age height weight};
```

IML responds:

```
Opening USER.CLASS(DATA)
```

Your INFILE command opens the CLASS.DAT file to get your data for IML to process:

```
> infile "class.dat";

Opening file class.dat
```

You use a DO loop to iterate the INPUT statement until end-of-file is reached; the APPEND command adds the current values to the output data set CLASS:

```
> do data;
>    input name $ sex $ age height weight;
>    append;
>    end;

* end-of-file for file class.dat
```

Finally, use the CLOSE command to close the data set:

```
> close class;

Closing USER.CLASS
NOTE: The data set USER.CLASS has 19 observations and 5 variables.
```

You now have a SAS data set USER.CLASS with 5 variables and 19 records. Now, try to look at the data set you just created. The USE command opens the data set for read access only.

```
> use class;

Opening USER.CLASS(DATA)
```

(Commands you enter later operate on this data set.)
Now issue two SHOW commands to investigate the data set contents:

```
> show datasets;

            DATA SET NAME
            USER    .CLASS         current input

> show contents;

            VAR NAME    TYPE    SIZE
               NAME     CHAR     8
               SEX      CHAR     1
               AGE      NUM      8
               HEIGHT   NUM      8
               WEIGHT   NUM      8
            Number of Observations: 19
```

Browsing and Listing Data Set Values

To look at the actual values in the data set, use the LIST command:

```
> list all;
```

OBS	NAME	SEX	AGE	HEIGHT	WEIGHT
1	JOYCE	F	11	51.3	50.5
2	THOMAS	M	11	57.5	85
3	JAMES	M	12	57.3	83
4	JANE	F	12	59.8	84.5
5	JOHN	M	12	59	99.5
6	LOUISE	F	12	56.3	77
7	ROBERT	M	12	64.8	128
8	ALICE	F	13	56.5	84
9	BARBARA	F	13	65.3	98
10	JEFFREY	M	13	62.5	84
11	CAROL	F	14	62.8	102.5
12	HENRY	M	14	63.5	102.5
13	ALFRED	M	14	69	112.5
14	JUDY	F	14	64.3	90
15	JANET	F	15	62.5	112.5
16	MARY	F	15	66.5	112
17	RONALD	M	15	67	133
18	WILLIAM	M	15	66.5	112
19	PHILIP	M	16	72	150

IML offers a variety of ways to list observations. When you want to list all observations in the data set, use the LIST command with the ALL keyword to indicate the range as shown above. Without a range specification, LIST lists the current observation:

```
> list;
```

OBS	NAME	SEX	AGE	HEIGHT	WEIGHT
19	PHILIP	M	16	72	150

Use LIST's POINT specification with an expression to list one or more specific observations:

```
> list point 5;
```

OBS	NAME	SEX	AGE	HEIGHT	WEIGHT
5	JOHN	M	12	59	99.5

```
> list point {2 4 9};
```

```
OBS NAME        SEX        AGE    HEIGHT     WEIGHT
------ ---------  ---  ---------- ---------  ---------
     2 THOMAS     M           11    57.5          85
     4 JANE       F           12    59.8        84.5
     9 BARBARA    F           13    65.3          98
```

And a more interesting case:

```
> p=(2 4 9);

                        P               1 rows     3 columns
                            2           4               9

> print p;

                        P
                        2           4               9

> list point p;

        OBS NAME        SEX        AGE    HEIGHT     WEIGHT
        ------ ---------  ---  ---------- ---------  ---------
             2 THOMAS     M           11    57.5          85
             4 JANE       F           12    59.8        84.5
             9 BARBARA    F           13    65.3          98
```

LIST shows the values for all the variables unless you limit the variable list with an expression in the VAR clause:

```
> list var(name sex);

                    OBS NAME        SEX
                    ------ ---------  ---
                         9 BARBARA  F

> list point p var (name age);

                    OBS NAME        AGE
                    ------ ---------  ---------
                         2 THOMAS         11
                         4 JANE           12
                         9 BARBARA        13

> v=(name sex age);

                    V               1 rows     3 columns
                    NAME SEX  AGE

> list var v;
```

```
     OBS NAME     SEX    AGE
     ------ -------- --- ----------
         9 BARBARA  F        13
```

Another feature on the LIST command is the WHERE clause, which allows you to specify conditions for selecting observations:

```
> list all var v where(sex="M");

            OBS NAME     SEX      AGE
            ------ -------- --- ----------
                2 THOMAS   M        11
                3 JAMES    M        12
                5 JOHN     M        12
                7 ROBERT   M        12
               10 JEFFREY  M        13
               12 HENRY    M        14
               13 ALFRED   M        14
               17 RONALD   M        15
               18 WILLIAM  M        15
               19 PHILIP   M        16

> list all where(age>13);

       OBS NAME     SEX      AGE     HEIGHT     WEIGHT
       ------ -------- --- ---------- ---------- ----------
           11 CAROL    F        14       62.8      102.5
           12 HENRY    M        14       63.5      102.5
           13 ALFRED   M        14         69      112.5
           14 JUDY     F        14       64.3         90
           15 JANET    F        15       62.5      112.5
           16 MARY     F        15       66.5        112
           17 RONALD   M        15         67        133
           18 WILLIAM  M        15       66.5        112
           19 PHILIP   M        16         72        150
```

If you want to find out which observations satisfy a WHERE condition, use the FIND command and specify a variable in which IML can store the observation numbers found:

```
> find all where(age>13) into p;

9 observations were found

> print p;

                                    P
                                   11
                                   12
                                   13
                                   14
                                   15
```

```
                                  16
                                  17
                                  18
                                  19


> list point p;

          OBS NAME       SEX       AGE      HEIGHT      WEIGHT

          ------ --------- ---  ---------- ---------- ---------
           11 CAROL       F        14        62.8       102.5
           12 HENRY       M        14        63.5       102.5
           13 ALFRED      M        14          69       112.5
           14 JUDY        F        14        64.3          90
           15 JANET       F        15        62.5       112.5
           16 MARY        F        15        66.5         112
           17 RONALD      M        15          67         133
           18 WILLIAM     M        15        66.5         112
           19 PHILIP      M        16          72         150


> find all where(age>14) into q;

5 observations were found

> print p q;

                            P         Q
                           11        15
                           12        16
                           13        17
                           14        18
                           15        19
                           16
                           17
                           18
                           19


> list point q;

          OBS NAME       SEX       AGE      HEIGHT      WEIGHT

          ------ --------- ---  ---------- ---------- ---------
           15 JANET       F        15        62.5       112.5
           16 MARY        F        15        66.5         112
           17 RONALD      M        15          67         133
           18 WILLIAM     M        15        66.5         112
           19 PHILIP      M        16          72         150
```

If you want to read data from variables in the SAS data set into IML variables, use READ and any of the options that LIST allows: range of observations, scope of variables, or WHERE clause conditions.

```
> read point q;

> show names;

                    AGE          5 rows    1 cols num    8
                    HEIGHT       5 rows    1 cols num    8
                    NAME         5 rows    1 cols char   8
                    P            9 rows    1 cols num    8
                    Q            5 rows    1 cols num    8
                    SEX          5 rows    1 cols char   1
                    V            1 rows    3 cols char   4
                    WEIGHT       5 rows    1 cols num    8
                    Number of matrices 8


> print name sex age height weight;

                 NAME     SEX       AGE      HEIGHT     WEIGHT
                 JANET     F         15       62.5      112.5
                 MARY      F         15       66.5      112
                 RONALD    M         15       67        133
                 WILLIAM   M         15       66.5      112
                 PHILIP    M         16       72        150


> read point 8;


> print name sex age height weight;

              NAME     SEX       AGE      HEIGHT     WEIGHT
              ALICE     F         13       56.5        84

> read all var(name height) where(height>62);

12 observations found

> print name height;

                         NAME          HEIGHT
                         ROBERT         64.8
                         BARBARA        65.3
                         JEFFREY        62.5
                         CAROL          62.8
                         HENRY          63.5
                         ALFRED         69
                         JUDY           64.3
                         JANET          62.5
                         MARY           66.5
                         RONALD         67
                         WILLIAM        66.5
                         PHILIP         72
```

You can take matrices of values and create a new SAS data set:

```
> create new var{name height};

Opening USER.NEW(DATA)


> append;

> close new class;

Closing USER.NEW
NOTE: The data set USER.NEW has 12 observations and 2 variables.
Closing USER.CLASS
```

Now try some special features of the WHERE clause to find values that begin with certain characters (the =: operator) or sound like certain values (the =* operator), or contain certain strings (the ? operator). You can avoid putting a VAR clause on each LIST statement if you first open the SAS data set CLASS to look only at the variable or variables of interest:

```
> use class var{name};

Opening USER.CLASS(DATA)

> list all;

                     OBS NAME
                     ------ --------
                       1 JOYCE
                       2 THOMAS
                       3 JAMES
                       4 JANE
                       5 JOHN
                       6 LOUISE
                       7 ROBERT
                       8 ALICE
                       9 BARBARA
                      10 JEFFREY
                      11 CAROL
                      12 HENRY
                      13 ALFRED
                      14 JUDY
                      15 JANET
                      16 MARY
                      17 RONALD
                      18 WILLIAM
                      19 PHILIP


> list all where(name=:"J");

                     OBS NAME
                     ------ --------
                       1 JOYCE
                       3 JAMES
```

```
                                    4  JANE
                                    5  JOHN
                                   10  JEFFREY
                                   14  JUDY
                                   15  JANET


    > list all where(name=:"JA");

                              OBS  NAME

                              ------  --------
                                 3  JAMES
                                 4  JANE
                                15  JANET


    > list all where(name=*"LOIS");

                              OBS  NAME

                              ------  --------
                                 6  LOUISE


    > list all where(name=*"PHILLIP");

                              OBS  NAME

                              ------  --------
                                19  PHILIP


    > list all where(name?"AL");

                              OBS  NAME

                              ------  --------
                                 8  ALICE
                                13  ALFRED
                                17  RONALD
```

The WHERE comparison objectives can also be matrices of values; in this case, the comparison is done on each element until a match is found:

```
    > list all where(name=*{alfred carol judy});

                              OBS  NAME

                              ------  --------
                                11  CAROL
                                13  ALFRED
                                14  JUDY


    > list all where(name=*{jon jan });

                              OBS  NAME

                              ------  --------
                                 4  JANE
                                 5  JOHN
```

The WHERE comparison is always of the form:

dsvar operator operand

where *dsvar* is a variable in the data set; *operator* is one of the following comparison operators:

< <= > >= = ^= ? ^? =: =*

and *operand* is a literal value, IML variable name, or expression in parentheses. Note that the left side refers to values on the data set, and the right side refers to IML values. You can rewrite the previous comparison as:

```
n = {jon jan};
list all where(name=*n);
```

You cannot use general comparisons involving more than one data set value in a single comparison; for example, you cannot do:

```
list all where(height-age>weight);
list all where(height>weight);
```

You could use the second command if WEIGHT were an IML variable instead of a variable from the data set.

To change a value in the CLASS data set, you open the data set with the EDIT command rather than USE to be able to read and write to it:

```
> close class;
> edit class;

Opening USER.CLASS(DATA)
```

The REPLACE command replaces the values of the variables and observations listed with the values of the same IML variables. Here you find JOHN's record and change his age to 13:

```
> list all where(name="JOHN");
```

OBS	NAME	SEX	AGE	HEIGHT	WEIGHT
5	JOHN	M	12	59	99.5

```
> age=13;
```

```
             AGE        1 rows   1 columns
                          13
```

```
> replace point 5 var {age};
```

```
> list point 5;
```

OBS	NAME	SEX	AGE	HEIGHT	WEIGHT
5	JOHN	M	13	59	99.5

You can READ the values and then REPLACE or even APPEND them:

```
> read point 5;

> age=18; height=62.; weight=99;
```

AGE	1 rows	1 columns
18		

HEIGHT	1 rows	1 columns
62		

WEIGHT	1 rows	1 columns
99		

```
> append;

> list point 20;
```

OBS	NAME	SEX	AGE	HEIGHT	WEIGHT
20	JOHN	M	18	62	99

```
> close class;
```

Closing USER.CLASS

To sort the data set, use the SORT command to identify the input data set, the output data set, and a BY clause naming the variable by which to sort:

```
> sort class out=class2 by height;
```

NOTE: The data set USER.CLASS2 has 20 observations and 5 variables.

```
> use class2;
```

Opening USER.CLASS2(DATA)

```
> list all;
```

OBS	NAME	SEX	AGE	HEIGHT	WEIGHT
1	JOYCE	F	11	51.3	50.5
2	LOUISE	F	12	56.3	77
3	ALICE	F	13	56.5	84
4	JAMES	M	12	57.3	83
5	THOMAS	M	11	57.5	85
6	JOHN	M	13	59	99.5
7	JANE	F	12	59.8	84.5
8	JOHN	M	18	62	99
9	JEFFREY	M	13	62.5	84
10	JANET	F	15	62.5	112.5

11	CAROL	F	14	62.8	102.5
12	HENRY	M	14	63.5	102.5
13	JUDY	F	14	64.3	90
14	ROBERT	M	12	64.8	128
15	BARBARA	F	13	65.3	98
16	MARY	F	15	66.5	112
17	WILLIAM	M	15	66.5	112
18	RONALD	M	15	67	133
19	ALFRED	M	14	69	112.5
20	PHILIP	M	16	72	150

Indexing the Data Set

Searching through a large data set for information about one or more specific records may take IML a long time since the procedure must read each record. You can reduce this search time to less than two seconds by first indexing the data set. The INDEX command builds a special file containing the values and record numbers of the indexed variables. After the index is built, later queries with WHERE clauses use the index to find the records more quickly:

```
> index name;
```

```
> list all where(name=:"JO");
```

OBS	NAME	SEX	AGE	HEIGHT	WEIGHT
6	JOHN	M	13	59	99.5
8	JOHN	M	18	62	99
1	JOYCE	F	11	51.3	50.5

Note that the retrieved records do not come out in order of the observation number in the data set (most recently sorted by WEIGHT), but rather in key order. If you want to find the next record in key order, then use the NEXTKEY range keyword:

```
> list nextkey;
```

OBS	NAME	SEX	AGE	HEIGHT	WEIGHT
13	JUDY	F	14	64.3	90

```
> list nextkey;
```

OBS	NAME	SEX	AGE	HEIGHT	WEIGHT
2	LOUISE	F	12	56.3	77

PART II: LANGUAGE GUIDE

SAS/IML™ Language Overview

SAS/IML™ Expressions

SAS/IML™ Programming Statements

SAS/IML™ Library Storage

SAS/IML™ Data Processing

SAS/IML™ File Access

SAS/IML™ Display Features

Detail Notes

## Chapter 6

SAS/IML™ Language Overview

SAS/IML Data and Variables

IML is a system in which the fundamental data entity is a 2-dimensional (row x column) numeric or character matrix. IML expressions deal with and yield matrix values. These values are stored in a workspace that is managed so that space can be recovered and reused as it becomes available. You can store a matrix value under a 1 to 8 character name. IML stores the name in a symbol table along with the attributes and location of the value. Because IML handles the names and values separately, it is possible to have names that do not have values or names associated with values that have different types and dimensions at different times. Usually, a name is associated with a value that is created from an expression in an assignment statement. See **Data in SAS/IML** in the chapter "SAS/IML Expressions" for more information.

Invoking the Procedure

To invoke IML under SAS you submit the PROC IML statement:

```
PROC IML;
```

You can use one option in the PROC statement:

WRKSIZE=*number*
    specifies the number of K (1024 bytes) of memory to allocate to the workspace. For example,

```
PROC IML WORKSIZE=30;
```

        The amount of workspace you can specify depends on the capacity of your computer and the products that are installed.

Basic Operation

IML is an interactive procedure. The procedure executes each statement as it is entered; almost all statements execute immediately.

If you want to delay the execution of a set of statements until you are finished with the set, you begin the set with a DO statement. IML delays execution until you enter a corresponding END statement.

If you want to store a set of statements for later execution, you can enclose the statements with START and FINISH statements. This creates a module that you can execute later with the RUN statement.

When you are ready to exit IML, enter the QUIT statement.

Statements Used with IML

The statements that control IML begin with a keyword and end in a semicolon(;). (The only exceptions are assignment statements.) All statements used with IML are executable programming statements; that is, they execute immediately as entered (except for START, FINISH, and QUIT).

IML statements are classified into the following groups:

- **Commands** perform special processing such as setting options, printing, and handling I/O.
- **Control statements** direct the flow of execution.
- **Assignment statements** and **calls** evaluate expressions and assign results to a name.

Commands   Each command performs a specific action. The syntax of a command is tailored to its application. Commands include:

RESET
        sets various options, such as linesize, default field width, or automatic printing.

SHOW
        shows various information, such as how much workspace is being used or what files are opened.

I/O commands
        perform operations on SAS data sets, such as READ, LIST, or APPEND.

File commands
        perform operations on external input and output files.

FREE
        frees a matrix of its values and returns memory to the available memory in the workspace.

PRINT
        prints values and messages.

STORE/LOAD
        store and retrieve values from matrix library storage on disk.

MATTRIB
        associates attributes with names.

Control statements   Control statements direct the flow of execution of the other statements in IML. The control statements in IML work similarly to those in other programming languages (such as the SAS DATA step). The control statements are

GOTO,LINK
> direct IML to jump to a statement with the given label and to continue execution of statements at that point.

PAUSE,RESUME
> direct IML to pause or resume execution.

STOP,ABORT
> stop the execution of an IML program.

IF-THEN/ELSE
> provide for the conditional execution of statements or statement groups (subject to the evaluation of a conditional expression).

DO/END
> provide a way to group statements to be executed as a unit, sometimes repetitively.

START,FINISH
> define a module.

RUN
> invokes a module.

RETURN
> returns from a LINK or to calling module.

Here are some examples of control statements:

```
DO I=1 TO N;
   IF X>3 THEN GOTO TROUBLE;
   ELSE DO;
      LINK SUB;
      RUN MOD;
      END;
   END;
```

Assignment and call statements Assignment statements perform calculations and manipulations in IML. An assignment is of the form:

result=expression;

The *expression* is composed of operands and operators that perform a set of operations on values. The expression yields a value that is stored in the *result* variable. IML declares and allocates variables automatically at execution.

Here are some examples of assignment statements:

```
I=1;
YEAR=1986;
PROFIT=REVENUES-EXPENSES;
z=sqrt(x**2+y**2);
a[i]=a[i]+x;
```

Call statements invoke a routine to do calculations or perform a service. They are often used in place of functions when the operation returns more than one result or, in some cases, no result:

```
CALL routine (arg1,arg2,...);
CALL routine;
```

SAS/IML™ Expressions

Data in SAS/IML

SAS/IML is a programming language in which the fundamental data entity is not a single numeric or character value, but a two-dimensional (row x column) numeric or character matrix. Elements in numeric matrices are stored as real double-precision, floating-point values. Elements in character matrices are stored as character strings with equal lengths ranging from 1 to 32767 characters long. A matrix is usually given a name and is stored by rows.

IML deals with expressions in terms of these matrices. For example, the expression A+B in IML adds the elements of the two matrices **A** and **B**.

The dimension of a matrix is described by the number of rows and columns. Thus, an m by n (m x n) matrix has m x n numbers arranged in m rows and n columns. In this manual matrices of dimensions

    1 x n are called row vectors
    n x 1 are called column vectors
    1 x 1 are called scalars.

Matrices can be unvalued; that is, they can exist even though they have not yet been set to a value. Also, the elements of a numeric matrix can be missing values (see **Missing Values**).

Matrix Names and Matrix Literals

Matrices are usually referred to by name. The rules for naming matrices are the same as for other SAS names: one to eight characters long, beginning with a letter or an underscore. Matrix names refer to matrices that have been set up by an assignment statement or command. A matrix assumes the dimensions of the result of an expression and can be redefined later with different dimensions.

A matrix literal is a matrix referred to as its values. If there is only one element, a matrix literal can be written directly as any of the following:

- a positive number, with or without decimal points, possibly in scientific notation (like 1E−5). IML treats minus signs before numbers as minus operators rather than signs, except when inside braces.
- a character string inside single quotes (') or double quotes("). It can contain either uppercase or lowercase letters, and the case will be preserved. If your string has embedded quotes, you must double them. For example, WORD='Can''t';.
- a period, representing a numeric missing value.

Here are some examples of literals:

```
X = 12;
x = 12.34;
x = .;            /* missing value */
a = 'Hi There';
b = "Hello";
```

If there are multiple elements, use braces { } to enclose the values. Inside the braces, values can be any of the following:

- a number, as above, but it can be negative by being prefixed by a minus sign (−)
- a period, representing a missing value
- a character string enclosed by either single or double quotes, as described above
- names, which will be converted to uppercase
- commas, which separate the rows of the matrix
- numbers in brackets, signifying repetition factors
- the following special characters:

      = * | ( )

Within the braces, the values must be all numeric or all character. If you use commas to create multiple rows, each row must have the same number of elements.

Below are some matrix literal examples. The statement

```
X={1 2, 3 4, 5 6};
```

assigns a 3-row by 2-column matrix literal to the matrix **X**:

$$\begin{bmatrix} 1 & 2 \\ 3 & 4 \\ 5 & 6 \end{bmatrix}.$$

Here are some further examples:

```
A={-23};                            /* single negative value */
B={-2.1 240, 2.2E3 4};              /* a 2-by-2 matrix */
addresses={"12 Main Street",
           "222 Broadway"  };       /* quoted strings */
names = {john jane jim };           /* names converted to uppercase */
model = {y = a b a*b };             /* names and special chars */
```

A matrix literal can be used in expressions wherever a matrix name is used. The IML statement

```
D=REPEAT(0,2,3);
```

is equivalent to the statements

```
A=0;
B=2;
C=3;
D=REPEAT(A,B,C);
```

For character matrix literals, the length of the string elements is determined from the longest string element. Shorter strings are extended with blanks. For example, the assignment of the literal:

```
A={'ABC', 'DEFG'};
```

results in **A** being a character matrix with 2 rows, 1 column, and with string length 4.

A repetition factor can be placed in brackets before a literal element to have the element repeated. For example,

```
D = {[3] 0 [2] 1};
```

is equivalent to

```
D = {0 0 0 1 1};
```

And

```
answer = {[3] "Yes" [2] "No"};
```

is equivalent to

```
answer = {"Yes" "Yes" "Yes" "No" "No"};
```

Assignment Statements

Assignment statements evaluate expressions and give a name to the resulting matrix. An assignment statement consists of a result variable, an equal sign (=), an expression to be evaluated, and a semicolon. Assignment statements have the following form:

result = *expression*;

The expression is evaluated and assigned to the result name. No special declaration or dimension specification of the resulting matrix is needed. The result automatically acquires the dimensions and values endowed to it by the expression.

Details on writing expressions are described in **Matrix Expressions**.

The statement

```
Y={4 5 6};
```

sets up a 1 x 3 numeric matrix named **Y**, whose elements are 4, 5, and 6.

The statement

```
A={8 5 3, 5 8 5, 3 5 8};
```

sets up a 3 x 3 matrix named **A**. In this statement, rows are separated by commas.

The statement

```
B=INV(A);
```

computes the inverse of matrix **A** and assigns that result to the matrix **B**.

CALL Statements

CALL statements invoke a routine to do calculations or perform some service. They are often used in place of functions when the operation returns more than one result or, in some cases, no result. The form of the CALL statement is

CALL *routine* (*argument1,argument2,...*);
CALL *routine*;

If you specify several arguments, use commas to separate them. If you specify both output results and input parameters as arguments, always specify the output results first. Also, when using arguments for output results, always use names rather than literals or expressions.

Matrix Expressions

Matrix expressions are a sequence of names, literals, operators, and functions that perform some calculation, evaluate some condition, or manipulate values.

Operators   IML provides prefix, postfix, and infix operators to be used in expressions involving matrices.

For example, the expression

−A

uses the prefix operator (−) in front of the operand A to reverse the sign of each element of matrix **A**.

The expression

A+B

uses the infix operator (+) between its operands A and B to add corresponding elements of matrices **A** and **B**.

The expression

A `

uses the postfix operator (`) after its operand A to produce the transpose of matrix **A**.

These matrix operators and others are shown in **Table 7.1** and are described in detail in the "SAS/IML Language Reference" chapter.

Compound expressions   In IML, you can write compound expressions involving several matrix operators and operands. For example, the statements

```
A=X+Y+Z;
A=X+Y*Z;
A=X/Y/Z;
A=X/(Y/Z);
```

are valid matrix assignment statements.

The following are rules for evaluating such expressions:

- Evaluation follows the order of operator precedence, according to the precedence table shown in **Table 7.1**. Group I has the highest priority; that is, Group I operators are evaluated first. Group II operators are evaluated after Group I operators, and so forth. For example,

    A=X+Y*Z

    first multiplies matrices **Y** and **Z** since the * operator has higher precedence than +. It then adds the result of this multiplication to the matrix **X**, and assigns the new matrix to **A**.
- If neighboring operators in an expression have equal precedence, the expression is evaluated from left to right, except for the highest priority operators. For example, the expression

    A=X / Y / Z

    first divides each element of matrix **X** by the corresponding element of matrix **Y**. Then, using the result of this division, it divides each element of the resulting matrix by the corresponding element of matrix **Z**. The operators in the highest group of precedence shown in **Table 7.1** are evaluated from right to left. For example,

    −X**2

is evaluated as

    −(X**2)   .

When multiple prefix or postfix operators are juxtaposed, precedence is determined by their order from inside to outside. For example,

$^\wedge-A$

is evaluated as $^\wedge(-A)$, and

A ` [I,J]

is evaluated as (A `)[I,J].
• All expressions enclosed in parentheses are evaluated first, using the two rules above. Thus, the IML statement

```
A=X / (Y/Z);
```

is evaluated by first dividing elements of matrix **Y** by **Z**, then dividing this result into **X**.

Table 7.1 Operator Precedence

Group I (highest priority)

^   `   subscripts   −(prefix)   ##   **

Group II

*   #   <>   ><   /   @

Group III

+   −

Group IV

|| //   :

Group V

<   <=   >   >=   =   ^=

Group VI

&

Group VII (lowest priority)

|

Functions   Functions are operations invoked by the name of the function rather than by special operator characters. Functions are expressed as the name of the function followed by a list of arguments enclosed in parentheses, with arguments separated by commas:

result=function (*argument1,argument2,...,argumentn*);

The arguments can be matrix names, literals, or expressions.

Scalar functions operate on each element of the matrix argument. If you use several arguments, they must all have the same dimensions (except for scalar values which are always permitted). These functions have the same form and function in IML as in the SAS DATA step, with the exception of the MAX, MIN, and SUM functions, which have different meanings in IML.

For example, to create a 10 x 1 matrix of random numbers, use

```
X=UNIFORM (REPEAT(0,10,1));
```

Other functions, such as INV, are unique to IML and are described in detail in the "SAS/IML Language Reference" chapter. They appear in alphabetical order along with the commands.

Elementwise binary extensions   The following operators are called elementwise binary operators because they work in an elementwise fashion, producing a result matrix from element-by-element operations on two argument matrices:

+	addition
−	subtraction
#	element multiplication
/	division
##	raise to power
<>	element maximum
><	element minimum
|	logical or
&	logical and
<	less than
<=	less than or equal to
>	greater than
>=	greater than or equal to
^=	not equal to
=	equal to
MOD(*m,n*)	modulo (remainder)

All these operators can also work in a one-to-many or many-to-one manner, as well as in an element-to-element manner; that is, they allow you to do things like add a scalar to a matrix, or divide a matrix by a scalar.

For example, the IML statement

```
X=X # (X>0);
```

replaces each negative element of the matrix **X** with zero. The expression (X>0) is a many-to-one operation that compares each element of **X** to 0 and creates a temporary matrix of results; a result matrix element is 1 when the expression is true and 0 when false. When the expression is true (the element is positive), the element is multiplied by one. When the expression is false (the element is negative or zero), the element is multiplied by zero.

Subscripts   Subscripts are special postfix operators placed in square brackets [ ] after a matrix operand. You can use subscripts to

- refer to a single element of a matrix
- refer to an entire row or column of a matrix
- refer to any submatrix contained within a matrix
- perform a reduction across rows or columns of a matrix.

Subscript operations are of the form:

operand[*rows, columns*]

where *rows* is an expression to select one or more rows from the operand, and *columns* selects one or more columns from the operand. The operand is usually a matrix name, but it can also be an expression or literal. The row or column arguments are scalars or vectors. In expressions, subscripts have the same high precedence as the transpose postfix operator (`). Note that when two subscripts are used, they are separated by a comma.

Here is an example:

```
X={1 2 3,
   4 5 6,
   7 8 9};
A=X[2,3];
```

The first statement above sets up the 3 x 3 matrix **X**. The next statement assigns to matrix **A** the element in the second row, third column of **X**. Thus, **A** is a 1 x 1 matrix whose only element has the value 6.

When you use two subscripts, the first selects the row, and the second the column. When you use one subscript, it looks up the elements in row major ordering (it looks down the rows). For example, the statement:

```
Y=X[5];
```

selects the 5th element of **X** counting along the rows. Since **X** is a 3 x 3 matrix, this element turns out to be the same as:

```
Y=X[2,2];
```

Entire row or column   To refer to an entire row or column of a matrix, write the subscript with the row or column number, omitting the other subscript but not the comma. For example, the statement

```
A=X[3,];
```

assigns the third row of **X** to **A**. The statement

```
B=X[,2];
```

assigns the second column of **X** to **B**. The statement

```
X[,1]={5, 6, 7};
```

changes the elements in the first column of **X** to 5, 6, and 7.

Submatrices   You can define submatrices within matrices with subscripts. For example, to refer to the matrix formed by the four elements in the upper right corner of matrix **X** above, use the statement

```
R=X[{1 2},{2 3}];
```

The first subscript, 1 2, selects the rows of **X** to be included in the new matrix **R**. The second subscript, 2 3, selects the columns to be included. Thus, the new matrix **R** is

$$\begin{bmatrix} 2 & 3 \\ 5 & 6 \end{bmatrix} .$$

Index vectors   You can often use index vectors generated by the : operator in subscripts. For example, the statement

```
Y=A[1:7,4];
```

is equivalent to

```
Y=A[{1 2 3 4 5 6 7}, 4];
```

and defines **Y** to be the 7 x 1 matrix formed from the first 7 elements of the fourth column of matrix **A**.

Note that the number of elements in the first subscript defines the number of rows in the new matrix; the number of elements in the second subscript defines the number of columns. For example, in the statement

```
P=C[{2 4 5},{1 3}];
```

the first subscript has 3 elements: 2, 4, and 5. The second subscript has 2 elements: 1 and 3. Thus, **P** has 3 rows and 2 columns.

The LOC function is often convenient for creating an index vector for a matrix that satisfies some condition. For example, the statements

```
I=LOC(X<0);
X[I]= 0;
```

find the positions of the negative elements of **X** and then set these elements to zero.

Expressions as subscripts   Subscripts can also contain other expressions whose results are either row or column vectors. For example, consider these statements:

```
A={3 1};
```

```
X={1 2 3,
   4 5 6,
   7 8 9};
M=X[2,A];
```

A is a row vector with 2 elements. It appears as a subscript in the the last statement, which can also be written as:

```
M=X[2,{3 1}];
```

Thus, **M** is a 1 x 2 matrix with the values:

$$\begin{bmatrix} 6 & 4 \end{bmatrix} .$$

If you use a noninteger value as a subscript, it is truncated to the next lower integer. Using a subscript value less than one or greater than the dimension of the matrix results in an error.

Subscript operators are general postfix operators that can be applied to any valid expression. For example,

```
(A+B)[1,2];
```

is a valid expression. This expression selects the element in the first row, second column of the matrix formed by the sum of matrices **A** and **B**.

Subscripted assignment   You can also assign values into a subscripted matrix. To do this, put the subscript expression after the result name in an assignment. Here is an example:

```
X={1 2 3,
   4 5 6,
   7 8 9};
X[1,3]=0;
```

The last statement inserts a value of 0 into the element in the first row, third column of **X**. The values of **X** are

$$\begin{bmatrix} 1 & 2 & 0 \\ 4 & 5 & 6 \\ 7 & 8 & 9 \end{bmatrix} .$$

Note that when subscripts are used on the left side of an equal sign, the matrix that is subscripted must already be defined and have values. You can insert a matrix of values into a submatrix of the result matrix as long as you specify matching numbers of columns and rows. For example, suppose that **G** is a 4 x 5 matrix and you want to insert **H**, a 3 x 2 matrix, into rows (1 3 4) and columns (2 3) of **G**.

```
G={1  2  3  4  5,
   6  7  8  9 10,
  11 12 13 14 15,
  16 17 18 19 20};
H={1111 1122,
   2211 2222,
   3311 3322};
```

The following statement

```
G[{1 3 4} ,{2 3}]=H;
```

produces the result in **G**:

$$
\begin{bmatrix}
1 & 1111 & 1122 & 4 & 5 \\
6 & 7 & 8 & 9 & 10 \\
11 & 2211 & 2222 & 14 & 15 \\
16 & 3311 & 3322 & 19 & 20
\end{bmatrix}.
$$

Subscripted assignment also allows you to insert a single value into a submatrix with multiple rows and columns. Continuing with the previous example, you can insert the value 99 into the submatrix with the following statement:

```
G[{1 3 4} ,{2 3}]=99;
```

The result in **G** is

$$
\begin{bmatrix}
1 & 99 & 99 & 4 & 5 \\
6 & 7 & 8 & 9 & 10 \\
11 & 99 & 99 & 14 & 15 \\
16 & 99 & 99 & 19 & 20
\end{bmatrix}.
$$

Subscript reduction operators   You can use reduction operators in place of values in subscripts to get reductions across all rows and columns.

Eight operators are available in IML subscript reduction:

+	addition
#	multiplication
<>	maximum
><	minimum
<:>	index of maximum
>:<	index of minimum
:	mean (different from SAS MATRIX)
##	sum of squares

For example, to get column sums of the matrix **X** (sum across the rows, which reduces the row dimension to 1), specify X[+,]. The elements in each column are added, and the new matrix consists of one row containing the column sums.

Since the second subscript was omitted in the example above, the column dimension was not changed. The first subscript (+) means that summation reduction takes place across the rows.

You can use these operators to reduce either rows, or columns, or both. When both rows and columns are reduced, the row reduction is done first.

For example, the expression A[+,<>] results in the maximum of the column sums. To get the sum of the row maxima, specify

A[,<>] [+,] .

A subscript such as A[[2 3] ,+] first selects the second and third rows of **A** and then finds the row sums of that matrix.

The following examples demonstrate how to use the operators for subscript reduction:

If

A={ 0 1 2,
    5 4 3,
    7 6 8 }

then

A[{2 3},+] yields   [12]   (row sums for rows 2 and 3)
                      [21]

A[+,<>] yields   [13]   (maximum of column sums)

A[<>,+] yields   [21]   (sum of column maxima)

A[,><] [+,] yields [9]   (sum of row minima)

A[,<:>] yields   [3]   (indices of row maxima)
                      [1]
                      [3]

A[>:<,] yields   [1 1 1] (indices of column minima)

A[:] yields   [4]   (mean of all elements)

Missing Values

An IML numeric element can have a special value called a "missing value" that indicates that the value is unknown or unspecified. (A matrix with missing values should not be confused with an empty or unvalued matrix; that is, a matrix with 0 rows and 0 columns.) A numeric matrix can have any mixture of missing and nonmissing values.

IML supports missing values in a limited way. Only common arithmetic operators recognize missing arguments and propagate them. Many mathematical operations do not distinguish between a missing value and their coded value.

Missing values are coded in the bit pattern of very large negative numbers on your personal computer. This is supported as a "NAN" code for I.E.E.E. standard floating-point arithmetic processors (like the 8087 and 80287) but regarded as large negative numbers by software floating-point processors.

In literals, a numeric missing value is specified as a single period. In data processing operations, you can add or delete missing values. All operations that move values around move missing values properly. The following arithmetic operators propagate missing values:

+	addition	−	subtraction
#	multiply	/	division
<>	max	><	min
mod	modulo	##	raise to power

The comparison operators treat missing values as large negative numbers. The logical operators treat missing values as zeros. The operators SUM, SSQ, MAX, and MIN check for and exclude missing values.

Chapter 8
SAS/IML™ Programming Statements

Conditionals
DO Groups
Jumping (Nonconsecutive Execution)
Stopping
Iteration
Module Definition and Execution
    Module nesting
    Modules with arguments
Suspended Execution with PAUSE, RESUME, and STOP
Break Interrupt

IML is a programming language. As a programming language it has many features that allow you to control the path of execution through the statements. The control statements in IML function in a similar way to the corresponding statements in the SAS DATA step. This chapter presents the following control features:

- conditionals
- DO groups
- jumping
- stopping
- iteration
- module definition and invocation
- pausing and resuming.

Each of the statements is described briefly below. They are described in greater detail in the "SAS/IML Language Reference" chapter.

Conditionals

To perform an operation conditionally, use an IF statement to test an expression. Alternative actions appear in a THEN clause or an ELSE statement. The form of the IF-THEN/ELSE statement is

    IF *expression* **THEN** *statement1;*
    ELSE *statement2;*

The ELSE statement is, of course, optional.
    The IF expression is evaluated first. If the expression evaluates as true (all values are nonzero and nonmissing), execution flows through the THEN alternative. If the expression is false, the ELSE statement, if present, is executed.
    The expression to be evaluated is often a comparison. For example,

```
IF MAX(A)<20 THEN P=0;
    ELSE P=1;
```

The IF statement results in the evaluation of the condition (MAX(A)<20). If the largest value found in matrix **A** is less than 20, P is set to 0. Otherwise, P is set to 1.

When the condition to be evaluated is a matrix expression, the result of the evaluation is another matrix. If all values of the result matrix are nonzero, the condition is true; if any element in the result matrix is zero, the condition is false. This evaluation is equivalent to using the ALL function.

For example, writing

```
IF X<Y THEN ...;
```

produces the same result as writing

```
IF ALL(X<Y) THEN ...;
```

You can nest IF statements within the clauses of other IF or ELSE statements. Any number of nesting levels is allowed. For example,

```
IF X=Y THEN IF ABS(Y)=Z THEN ...;
```

Caution The expressions

```
IF A^=B THEN...;
```

and

```
IF ^(A=B) THEN...;
```

are valid, but the THEN clause in each case is only executed when all corresponding elements of **A** and **B** are unequal.

Evaluation of the expression

```
IF ANY(A^=B) THEN ...;
```

requires only one element of **A** and **B** to be unequal for the expression to be true.

DO Groups

A set of statements can be treated as a unit by putting them into a DO group, which starts with a DO statement and ends with an END statement. DO groups have the following form:

DO;
    statements...
    END;

The two principal uses of DO groups are

- to group a set of statements so that they are not executed immediately.
- to group a set of statements for a conditional clause.

For the IF/THEN-ELSE conditionals, DO groups behave as units for either THEN or ELSE clauses so that you can perform many statements as part of the conditional action. For example,

```
IF expression THEN DO;
    statements...
    END;
ELSE DO;
    statements...
    END;
```

DO groups can be nested to any depth; that is, you can have one DO group inside another, and that one inside yet another, and so forth.

It is good practice to indent the statements in a DO group as shown above so that their position indicates the level of nesting.

Jumping (Nonconsecutive Execution)

During normal execution, statements are executed one after another. The GOTO and LINK statements instruct IML to jump from one part of the program to another. The place to which execution jumps is identified by a label, which is a name followed by a colon placed before any executable statement. You can instruct IML to jump by using either

GOTO label;

or

LINK label;

along with

label: statement;

and, perhaps,

RETURN;

The GOTO and LINK statements are not often used since you can usually write more understandable programs by using other features, such as DO groups for conditionals, iterative DO groups for looping, and module invocation for subroutine calls.

The GOTO and LINK statements are also limited to being inside a module or DO group since they must be able to resolve the referenced label within the current unit of statements.

Both GOTO and LINK instruct IML to jump immediately to the labeled statement. The LINK statement, however, reminds IML where it jumped from so that execution can be returned there if a RETURN statement is encountered. The GOTO statement does not have this feature.

Here are two examples showing how GOTO and LINK work:

```
DO;                                 |  DO;
   IF X<0 THEN GOTO NEGATIVE;       |     IF X<0 THEN LINK NEGATIVE;
   Y=SQRT(X);                       |     Y=SQRT(X);
   PRINT Y;                         |     PRINT Y;
   STOP;                            |     STOP;
NEGATIVE:                           |  NEGATIVE:
   PRINT "Sorry, X is negative";    |     PRINT "Using Abs. value of negative X";
   STOP;                            |     X=ABS(X);
END;                                |     RETURN;
                                    |  END;
```

LINK provides a way of calling sections of code as if they were subroutines. The LINK statement calls the routine. The routine begins with the label and ends with a RETURN statement. LINK statements can be nested within other LINK statements to any level.

A RETURN statement without an outstanding LINK is a return from a called module, or if not in a module, it is executed just like the STOP statement (described below).

Although matrix symbols are shared across modules, statement labels are not. Therefore, all GOTO statement labels and LINK statement labels must be local to the module.

Stopping

The statements that cause execution to stop are the STOP, ABORT, and PAUSE statements. The QUIT statement is also a stopping statement, but QUIT immediately removes you from the IML environment, while the other stopping statements can be performed in the context of a program. Below are descriptions of STOP, ABORT, PAUSE, and RESUME:

STOP   stops execution and returns you to immediate mode, where IML continues to process new statements that you enter.

PAUSE   stops execution (like the STOP statement) but remembers where it stopped so that you can resume execution with a RESUME statement.

ABORT   stops execution and exits from IML much like a QUIT statement, except that it is executable and programmable.

RESUME   resumes execution after a PAUSE, or from an interrupt, as described below.

Iteration

The DO statement also serves the feature of iteration; that is, with a DO statement you can repeatedly execute a set of statements until some condition stops the execution. A DO statement is iterative if you specify any of the following iteration clauses:

DATA

variable = *start* TO *stop* <BY *increment*>

WHILE(*expression*)

UNTIL(*expression*)

The clauses determine when to stop the repetition. A DO statement can have any combination of these four iteration clauses, but they must be specified in the order given above.

The DATA keyword specifies that iteration is to stop when an end-of-file condition occurs due to some I/O operation. See the chapters "SAS/IML Data Processing" and "SAS/IML File Access." IML exits from the group immediately upon encountering the end-of-file condition, rather than exiting after tests are performed at the top or bottom of the loop.

The *variable* sequence specification assigns the *start* value to the given variable initially. This value is then incremented by the *increment* value (or by 1 if the BY increment is not specified) until it is greater than or equal to the *stop* value. (If the *increment* is negative, then the iterations stop when the value is less than or equal to the *stop* value).

The WHILE clause causes an expression to be evaluated at the beginning of each loop, with repetition continuing until the value is false (that is, when it contains a zero or missing value).

The UNTIL clause is like the WHILE clause except that it is evaluated at the bottom of the loop.

See the DO description in the "SAS/IML Language Reference" chapter for examples and further details.

Module Definition and Execution

Modules are used in IML for

- storing statements to be executed later, that is, for postponing execution.
- creating groups of statements that can be resolved as a unit.
- creating groups of statements that can be invoked as a unit from a variety of places in the program, that is, making a subroutine.
- creating a separate (symbol-table) environment.

The START and FINISH statements define the module. The RUN statement executes the module. The syntax for creating and executing a module is

START;

or

START *name*;

or

START *name* (*variable*,...);

.
.
.

FINISH;

.
.
.

RUN;

or

   RUN *name*;

or

   RUN *name* (*expressions*,...);

The module begins with a START statement and ends with a FINISH statement. If no name appears in the start statement, the name of the module defaults to MAIN. If no arguments are given, the routine uses the same set of variables (symbol table) as the immediate environment. If arguments are given, the routine creates its own local environment for variables (symbol table). The RUN statement must have arguments corresponding to the ones defined for the module it is invoking. A module can call other modules provided that it never calls itself recursively.

Module nesting The specification of statements for a module can be interrupted to specify statements for another module by nesting the statements with START/FINISH statements. Each module is collected independently of the others. For example,

```
START A;
  RESET PRINT;

  START B;
    A=A+1;
    FINISH;

  RUN B;
  RUN B;
  FINISH;

RUN A;
```

First IML starts collecting statements for a module called A. In the middle of this module it recognizes the start of a new module called B. It saves its current work on A and collects B until the first FINISH statement. Then it finishes collecting A. Thus, it behaves the same as if B were collected before A.

```
START B;
  A=A+1;
  FINISH;
START A;
  RESET PRINT;
  RUN B;
  RUN B;
  FINISH;
RUN A;
```

(Indentation is used to reflect the nesting.)

Nesting is useful in designing modules that %INCLUDE code that contains subroutines.

Modules with arguments Modules without arguments share the same symbol table as the immediate statements. Therefore, you can refer to the same matrix values from each module. However, sometimes you want a module to use its own symbol table, independent of the caller's symbol table except for parameters.

You can specify modules that have their own symbol table. Parameters are pushed into a parameter stack in the RUN statement and are passed to the new symbol table in the argument clause of the START statement. When the module returns, the old symbol table is restored, and the parameter matrices are returned to the caller's symbol table under the original names. For example,

```
START A(X,Y,Z);
    .
    .
    .
FINISH;


RUN A(XX,YY,ZZ);
```

The parameter-passing convention is call-by-reference. Parameter names used in subroutines refer directly to the argument matrices of the RUN statement. In the following example the use of **X** and **Y** in the subroutine S does not alter the values of the matrices **X** and **Y** unless one of them is the second argument of the subroutine:

```
X=1; Y=2;
START S (X,Y);
    Y=2#X;
    FINISH;
RUN S(X,A); *--- A=2#X---;
RUN S(Y,B); *--- B=2#Y---;

*---X AND Y REMAIN UNCHANGED---;

RUN S(Y,X); *--- X=2#Y---;

*---X HAS NOW BEEN CHANGED---;
```

Suspended Execution with PAUSE, RESUME, and STOP

Suppose that you want to be able to stop in the middle of a module, do some calculations, and then resume execution of the module. The PAUSE statement:

- stops execution of the module.
- saves the calling chain so that execution can be resumed later.
- prints a pause message that you can specify.
- puts you in immediate mode so you can enter more commands.

The RESUME statement allows you to continue execution at the place where the most recent PAUSE statement was executed.

You can use the STOP statement as an alternative to RESUME to remove the paused states and return to a clean immediate environment.

The syntax for these statements is

PAUSE;

or

PAUSE *expression*;

RESUME;

STOP;

You can specify an operand in the PAUSE statement to print a message as the pause prompt. If no operand is specified, IML prints the following default message:

```
paused in module XXX
```

where XXX is the name of the module containing the pause. Examples of pause operand are

```
PAUSE "Please enter an assignment for X, then enter RESUME;";

MSG="Please enter an assignment for X, then enter RESUME;";
PAUSE MSG;
```

When you use these statements, you should be aware of the following details:

- PAUSE in immediate mode stops execution, but execution cannot be resumed by a RESUME statement.
- IML diagnoses an error if you execute a RESUME without any pauses outstanding.
- You can execute and define new modules while paused from other modules.
- You cannot reenter or redefine an active (paused) module; this gives you an error for "recursive module execution."
- In paused mode, you can run another module that in turn pauses; the paused environments are stacked.
- You can put a RESUME statement inside a module. For example, if you are paused in module A, then run module B, which executes a RESUME statement. Execution is resumed in module A and does not return to module B.
- If you pause in a subroutine module that has its own symbol table, then the immediate mode during the pause uses this symbol table rather than the global one. You must use RESUME or STOP to get back to the immediate symbol table environment.

Break Interrupt

If you set the BREAK option, IML checks for the occurrence of a break interrupt, whereupon it behaves as if a PAUSE statement had been executed. Breaks are posted when the CNTL-BREAK keys are pressed, then IML tests for the occurrence of a break between each statement executed. Some commands, particularly I/O and PRINT commands test for break at each line or record encountered so that long operations can be interrupted.

## Chapter 9

SAS/IML™
Library Storage

RESET STORAGE= Option
SHOW STORAGE Command
STORE Command
LOAD Command
REMOVE Command

IML software can store values of matrices in a special library storage on disk for later retrieval. The library storage feature allows you to

- save work for a later session
- keep records of work
- conserve space by saving large, intermediate results for later use
- communicate data to other applications through the library
- store and retrieve data generally.

RESET STORAGE= Option

To specify the name of the library, use the STORAGE= feature of the RESET statement:

RESET STORAGE= "*member*";

or

RESET STORAGE= "*libref.member*";

or in general

RESET STORAGE= *operand*;

where the *operand* is either a literal, the name of a character-valued matrix, or an expression in parentheses.

IML storage libraries are specially structured SAS files that are located in a SAS data library. IML maintains the organization of these files, and you cannot use data set utility procedures to examine their contents.

You specify a storage library using a one- or two-level name: *libref* is the name of the SAS data library, and *member* is the name of the IML storage library. The default *libref* is the previous libref, which initially is SASUSER. The default member is IMLSTORE.

Each time you specify STORAGE=, the previously opened library is closed before the new one is opened.

You can have any number of libraries, but you can have only one open at a time. A SAS data library can contain many IML storage libraries, and an IML storage library can contain many IML matrices.

On PC DOS, SAS names the file "*member.SML*".

SHOW STORAGE Command

To find out what is currently in the library, use the STORAGE operand of the SHOW command:

SHOW STORAGE;

This gives a simple list of the names of the items in the library.

STORE Command

To save a matrix in the library, use the STORE command:

STORE *names*;

or

STORE;

If you do not specify a name, then IML saves all currently active matrices.

LOAD Command

To bring matrices from the library back into the IML active workspace, use the LOAD command:

LOAD *names*;

or

LOAD;

If you do not specify a name, IML loads all matrices stored in the library.

REMOVE Command

To remove a matrix from the library, use the remove command:

REMOVE *names*;

SAS/IML™ Data Processing

Introduction

With IML data processing commands, you have a complete set of tools with which to manipulate data in SAS data sets. These tools can be used for a variety of applications:

- large sequential data processing work
- quick queries
- transaction processing
- support for programming systems.

Overview of Commands

IML has a set of commands that operate on SAS data sets. A variable in IML corresponds to a field in the data set. The values in IML variables correspond to values in different records in the data set. IML data processing commands are described briefly below:

USE

    opens a SAS data set for read access.

EDIT

    opens a SAS data set for read and write access.

CREATE

    opens a new SAS data set.

CLOSE

    closes a SAS data set.

SETIN

    selects an open data set for input.

SETOUT
>   selects an open data set for output.

SHOW DATASETS
>   shows data sets that are currently active.

SHOW CONTENTS
>   shows contents of the current input data set.

RESET DEFLIB=*operand*
>   specifies the default libname to be used when no libname is specified.

RESET CASE
>   specifies that IML not convert comparison strings to uppercase.

RESET SPILL
>   for large data sets, is used in order to allow the entire data set to be read in. Disk space instead of memory is used as a work area.

LIST
>   lists the records.

READ
>   reads the data into IML variables.

REPLACE
>   writes data back into a data set.

APPEND
>   adds records to the end of the data set.

FIND
>   finds the records satisfying the specified conditions.

DELETE
>   marks records as deleted.

FORCE
>   forces data to a data set.

PURGE
>   purges all deleted records from a SAS data set.

SORT
>   sorts a data set.

SUMMARY
>   computes summary statistics for numeric variables of a data set.

INDEX
>   indexes a data set.

Opening SAS Data Sets

You must open a data set before you can access it. There are three ways to open a SAS data set:

1. To simply read from an existing data set, submit a USE command to open it for read access. With read access you can use the LIST, READ, and FIND commands to access data.
2. To read and write to an existing data set, use the EDIT command. This command enables you to use both the reading commands (LIST, READ, and FIND) and the writing commands (REPLACE, APPEND, DELETE, and PURGE).
3. To create a new data set, use CREATE instead of EDIT to open a new data set for both output and input.

Naming Data Sets

The USE, EDIT, and CREATE commands take as their first operand the data set name. This name can either have one or two levels. If it is a two-level name, the first level refers to the libref that controls where the data set is located; the second name is the data set name. If the libref is WORK, the data set is put into a directory for temporary data sets; these are automatically deleted at the end of the session. Other librefs are associated with other directories via a LIBNAME statement.

If you only specify a single name, then IML supplies a default libref. At the beginning of an IML session, the default libref is blank, which denotes 'USER'. 'USER' is defined as a libref or 'WORK' otherwise. However, you can reset this by using the following command:

```
RESET DEFLIB='name';
```

Current Data Set

The data processing commands work on the current data set. This feature makes it unnecessary for you to specify the data set as an operand each time. There are two current data sets, one for input and one for output. IML makes a data set the current one as it is opened. You can also make a data set current by using two setting commands, SETIN and SETOUT.

USE, SETIN
        make the data set current input.

CREATE, SETOUT
        make the data set current output.

EDIT
        makes the data set both current input and current output.

If you issue USE, EDIT, or CREATE commands for a data set that is already open, the data set is made the current data set.

To find out which data sets are open and which are current input and current output data sets, use the SHOW DATASETS command.

Specifying Observations: the RANGE Operand

The first operand on access commands is usually a RANGE operand to specify the observations to process.

RANGE Keyword	Meaning
ALL	all observations
CURRENT	current observation
NEXT	next observation
AFTER	all observations after current one
POINT operand	observation number(s) specified by operand.

For example,

```
LIST ALL;
```

lists the whole data set.

```
LIST NEXT;
```

lists the next observation.

The POINT operand can be either a single number, a set of numbers in braces, a name of a matrix containing observation numbers, or an expression in parentheses. For example,

`LIST POINT 10;`	observation 10
`LIST POINT {10 25};`	observations 10 and 25
`LIST POINT N;`	observation N; N has a single array value
`LIST POINT (20:25);`	observations 20-25
`LIST POINT ((20:25)` `||(30:35));`	observations 20-25; 30-35

If the range is not specified, the default ranges are

Statement	Default Range
LIST	current
READ	current
FIND	all
REPLACE	current
APPEND	(always at end)
DELETE	current

The current range is set by the last operation that performed I/O. If you want to set the current observation without doing any I/O, use the SETIN (or SETOUT) statement with the POINT operand. For example,

```
SETIN A POINT 20;
```

Note that FIND sets current range, including multiple observation ranges.

After a data set is opened initially, the current observation is set to zero. If you attempt to list or read the current observation, it converts the current observation to 1. Thus,

```
LIST NEXT;
```

and

```
LIST CURRENT;
```

both list observation 1 initially.

Specifying a Set of Variables: the VAR Clause

You can specify a set of variables to work with by using the VAR clause with an operand specifying the names of the variables. This is also called the "scope" clause. The keyword VAR is followed by either a matrix literal of names, a name of a character matrix containing the names, or an expression in parentheses yielding the names. Also, the special keywords _ALL_, _CHAR_, and _NUM_ are available to use instead of the VAR clause. For example,

```
LIST VAR "X";                    X in double-quoted literal
LIST VAR 'X';                    X in single-quoted literal
LIST VAR {X Y};                  X and Y in matrix literal
NAMES={X Y};
LIST VAR NAMES;                  matrix containing names X and Y
MORE={W Z};
LIST VAR (NAMES||MORE);          expression yielding X, Y, W, and Z
LIST;                            all variables in the default scope
LIST VAR _ALL_;                  all variables
LIST VAR _NUM_;                  all numeric variables
LIST VAR _CHAR_;                 all character variables
```

You can use the VAR clause in the following statements:

USE	limits which variables are accessed.
EDIT	limits which variables are accessed.
CREATE	specifies the variables to go in the data set.
LIST	specifies which variables to list.
READ	specifies which variables to read.
REPLACE	specifies which variables to replace.
APPEND	specifies which variables to append.

The WHERE Clause

WHERE clauses specify the subset of the range for IML to process. The WHERE clause consists of one or more comparatives joined by logical operators. Comparatives are of the form

variable op value

or

variable op (expression)

or

variable op var

where

variable	refers to a variable on the file.
op	refers to a comparison operator.
value	is a literal value.
var	refers to the current value of an IML variable.

The comparison operators are presented below:

Operator	Comments
<	less than
<=	less than or equal to
=	equal to
^=	not equal to
>	greater than
>=	greater than or equal to
?	contains the value
^?	does not contain the value
=:	starts with the value
=*	sounds like.

The following operators can be used with a matrix of values as well as a single value. In this case it scans the matrix to find a matching value:

```
=   ^=   ?   ^?   =:   =*
```

The logical expressions are constructed:

clause & *clause*   (AND clause)
clause | *clause*   (OR clause)

where a *clause* is either a comparison, a parenthesized clause, or a logical expression clause using operator precedence.

For example, to list where NAME contains the value "Smith", use the following statement:

```
LIST ALL WHERE(NAME= "Smith");
```

To list where LASTNAME is either Smith, Jones, or Johnson, use the following statement:

```
LIST ALL WHERE( LASTNAME = "Smith"
              | LASTNAME = "Jones"
              | LASTNAME = "Johnson");
```

However, this statement is more concise:

```
LIST ALL WHERE(LASTNAME = ("Smith" "Jones" "Johnson"));
```

The statement above is equivalent to:

```
FINDNAME = ("Smith" "Jones" "Johnson");
LIST ALL WHERE(LASTNAME=FINDNAME);
```

The following example finds records for customers named Smith whose accounts are overdrawn, lists pertinent variable values, reads the values into IML variables, and then appends the data to another SAS data set:

```
USE     ACCOUNTS  VAR (NAME ACCTNUM BALANCE);
FIND    INTO  P WHERE(NAME="SMITH" & BALANCE<0);
LIST    POINT P;
READ    POINT P;

EDIT    OVERS VAR (NAME ACCCTNUM BALANCE);
APPEND  ;
```

SAS DATA SET
⟹ matrix

Data Processing of Entire Matrices

Sometimes you may want to read the contents of a SAS data set into a single matrix, for example, to compute correlation estimates from a set of data. You can perform data processing on entire matrices using the FROM and INTO clauses of the READ, APPEND, and CREATE statements.

For example, the statement

```
READ ALL INTO X;
```

creates a matrix **X** with one column for each numeric variable on the data set and a row for each observation. Use the RANGE, VAR, and WHERE clauses as usual to select a subset of variables and observations.

The statement

```
READ ALL VAR _CHAR_ INTO X;
```

reads only character variables into **X**.

The statement

```
APPEND FROM X;
```

adds observations to the end of a data set. The columns of **X** become the first *ncol* variables of the same type as **X** where *ncol* is the number of columns in **X**. **Each row of X** creates a new observation.

The statement

```
CREATE SASdataset FROM X;
```

creates a SAS data set with *ncol* variables, all with the data characteristics of the matrix **X**. **X** must exist and have values.

You can specify a COLNAME matrix with CREATE and READ as shown below:

```
CREATE SASdataset FROM X [COLNAME=C];
READ INTO X [COLNAME=C];
```

Used with CREATE, the COLNAME matrix defines a set of variable names to be used for the columns of **X** in the new data set. When there is no COLNAME matrix, the variables are named COL1, COL2, ..., COLn. Used with READ, the COLNAME operand names a matrix to contain the names of the data set variables that become the columns of **X**.

You can also specify a ROWNAME matrix in CREATE, APPEND, and READ. The ROWNAME operand is a matrix of descriptive row titles. The name of the matrix must always correspond to the name of a character variable in the data set. When you APPEND to a data set created by the statement

```
CREATE SASdataset FROM X [ROWNAME=R];
```

the ROWNAME matrix of APPEND should be the same matrix used in CREATE,

```
APPEND FROM X [ROWNAME=R];
```

Used with READ, the ROWNAME operand names a character variable in the data set that contributes its values to a matrix of the same name. This new matrix has one column and *nrow* rows where *nrow* is the number of observations in the range.

Note that the VAR clause is incompatible with the FROM clause but not with the INTO clause.

End of File

If you try to read past the end of a data set or point to an observation greater than the number of observations in the data set, you create an end-of-file condition. IML prints a message on the log. If end of file occurs while inside a DO DATA iteration group, IML transfers control to the next statement outside the current DO DATA group.

```
USE SAVE.A;
   SUM=0;
DO DATA;
   READ NEXT VAR(X);
   SUM=SUM+X;
   END;
```

Indexing SAS Data Sets

If you frequently want to search a data set for values of certain variables, indexing can facilitate your searches considerably. To index a data set, open it and issue an index command for the variables you want to index. For example,

```
EDIT SAVE.MAILLIST;
INDEX NAME SSN;
```

This creates a companion index file (called MAILLIST.SNX) containing the values and observation numbers of the indexed variables in a form convenient for searching (technically known as a *b*-tree). Any number of variables can be indexed for each SAS data set.

Once you have indexed a data set, IML uses this index whenever a search is conducted with respect to the indexed variables. This means that an inquiry that may take a minute without indexes takes only a few seconds after indexing.

After you index a data set, IML keeps the indexes updated whenever you change values in indexed variables. You must take care that if you delete the data set you also delete the index. If you find a way to modify the data set by recreating it or by using PROC SORT, you must delete the index file yourself; otherwise, IML may try to use it because IML cannot tell that it is an invalid index.

Indexing is most useful for cases when you want to retrieve a few records from a large data set.

Deleted Observations

An observation in a SAS data set can be marked as deleted. A deleted observation is still physically in the file and still has an observation number, but it is excluded from processing. The deleted observations appear as gaps in the listings of the file by observation number.

Use the DELETE command to delete an observation. For example,

Code	Comment
`DELETE;`	delete current observation
`DELETE POINT 12;`	delete observation 12
`DELETE ALL WHERE (AGE>12);`	delete all observations where the condition is true

If a file accumulates a number of observations marked as deleted, you can clean out these observations by grouping the non-deleted observations together. Use the PURGE command to do this. For example,

```
EDIT SAVE.CLASS;
PURGE;
```

See the **PURGE Statement** in the "SAS/IML Language Reference" chapter for more information.

Sorting SAS Data Sets

The observations in a SAS data set can be ordered (sorted) by specific key variables. To sort a SAS data set, close the data set if it is currently opened, and issue a SORT command for the variables by which you want the observations to be ordered. Specify an output data set name if you want to keep the original data set. For example, the statement

```
SORT SAVE.MAILLIST OUT=SAVE.SORTMAIL BY NAME;
```

creates a new SAS data set SORTMAIL. The new data set has the observations from the data set MAILLIST, reordered by the variable NAME.

The statement,

```
SORT SAVE.MAILLIST BY NAME;
```

also sorts the data set MAILLIST by the variable NAME. However, at the completion of SORT, the original data set is replaced by the sorted data set.

You can specify as many key variables as needed, and, optionally, each variable can be preceded by the key word DESCENDING, which denotes that the variable that follows is to be sorted in descending order.

Summary Statistics

Summary statistics on the numeric variables of a SAS data set can be obtained with the SUMMARY command. These statistics can be based on subgroups of the data by using the CLASS clause in the SUMMARY command. The SAVE option in the OPT clause enables you to save the computed statistics in matrices for later perusal. For example, the IML statements

```
USE SAVE.CLASS;
SUMMARY VAR {HEIGHT WEIGHT} CLASS {SEX} STAT{MEAN STD} OPT {SAVE};
```

give the mean and standard deviation of the variables HEIGHT and WEIGHT for the two subgroups (male and female) of the data set CLASS. Since the SAVE option is set, the statistics of the variables are stored in matrices under the name of the corresponding variables, with each column corresponding to a statistic requested and each row corresponding to a subgroup. Two other vectors, SEX and _NOBS_, are created. The vector SEX contains the two distinct values of the class variable SEX used in forming the two subgroups. The vector _NOBS_ has the number of observations in each subgroup defined by the above.

Note that the combined mean and standard deviation of the two subgroups are displayed but are not saved.

More than one class variable can be used, in which case a subgroup is defined by the combination of the values of the class variables.

Data Set Maintenance Functions

IML provides two functions and two call routines to perform data set maintenance:

DATASETS function
> obtains members in a data library. This function returns a character matrix containing the names of the SAS data sets in a library.

CONTENTS function
> obtains variables in a member. This function returns a character matrix containing the variable names for the SAS data set specified by libname and memname. The variable list is returned in alphabetical order.

RENAME routine
> renames a SAS data set. This routine renames a SAS data set member in a specified library.

DELETE routine
> deletes (erases) a SAS data set. This routine deletes a SAS data set member in a specified library.

Note that the arguments to these functions and call routines are character matrices whose values are the library name and member name. To use the library name or member name explicitly, you must enclose them in either single or double quotation marks. See **DATASETS Function, CONTENTS Function, RENAME CALL**, and **DELETE Subroutine** in the "SAS/IML Language Reference" chapter. Other functions, statements, and routines useful in data set maintenance are listed below:

SORT   sorts a data set by one or more variables.

INDEX   builds an index for a variable.

See **SORT Statement** and **INDEX Statement** in the "SAS/IML Language Reference" chapter.

Similarities and Differences with the SAS DATA Step

If you want to remain in the IML environment and continue to do data processing (such as the SAS DATA step), you need only learn the basic differences between IML and the DATA step.

1. In IML, you must explicitly set up all your variables with the right attributes before you start the DATA step. In the DATA step the variable attributes are determined from context across the whole step.
2. In IML, you start with a CREATE statement instead of a DATA statement.
3. In IML, you must use an APPEND statement to output an observation; in the DATA step you either use an OUTPUT statement or let the DATA step output it automatically.
4. In IML, you iterate with a DO DATA loop. In the DATA step the iterations are implied.
5. In IML you have to close the data sets with a CLOSE statement unless you plan to leave the IML environment with a QUIT command. The DATA step closes the data set automatically at the end of the step.
6. The DATA step usually executes faster than IML.

In short, the DATA step treats the problem with greater simplicity, allowing shorter programs. However, IML has more flexibility because it is both interactive and has a powerful matrix-handling capability. Consider the following DATA step and equivalent IML code:

DATA step code:

```
DATA SAVE.B;
   SET SAVE.A;
   Y=X+1;
   IF STATE='IL';
```

Equivalent IML code:

```
STATE="..";
CREATE SAVE.B VAR( X Y STATE );
USE SAVE.A;
DO DATA;
   READ NEXT;
   Y=X+1;
   IF STATE="IL" THEN APPEND;
   END;
CLOSE SAVE.A SAVE.B;
```

SAS/IML™ File Access

Introduction

IML provides statements to read and write to external files. These files contain text or binary information in a format familiar to you, but not necessarily familiar to IML. This is in contrast to SAS data sets, which are specialized files whose structure is already known to the SAS System.

The statements used to access files are very similar to the corresponding statements in the SAS DATA Step. They are

INFILE	opens or points to a file for input (makes it the current input file).
INPUT	inputs records, reading values into IML variables.
FILE	opens or points to a file for output (makes it the current output file).
PUT	outputs records, putting values from IML variables.
CLOSEFILE	closes a file.

File Naming

There are two ways to refer to an input or output file: filepath and filename. The filepath is the name as known to the operating system. In PC/DOS the filepath can include the drive, the directory path, the name, and the extension of the file. The filename is a SAS reference to the file indirectly through a connection made with the FILENAME statement. You can specify a file in either way on the FILE and INFILE statements. To specify a filename as the operand, just give the name as the operand. The name must be one already connected to a filepath by a previously issued FILENAME statement. There are, however, two filenames that are recognized by IML: LOG and PRINT. These refer to the standard output streams for all SAS sessions. To specify a filepath, put it in quotes, or specify an expression yielding the filepath in parentheses.

For example,

```
INFILE "mydata.dat";            by literal filepath

FILENAME IN 'mydata.dat';       establish filename IN
INFILE IN;                      refer to file through filename

IN = 'a:mydata.dat';
INFILE (IN);                    by expression of filepath

FILE PRINT;                     special filename for standard print output

FILE LOG;                       special filename for log output
```

When the filepath is specified, there is a limit of thirty characters to the operand.

Text Files and Binary Files

Most files that you input can be called "text" files, which means that they can be edited and displayed without any special program. Text files on most host environments have special characters used to separate one record from the next. (To be precise, PC/DOS uses the two-character sequence: carriage-return "CR" Hex 0D, then linefeed "LF" Hex 0A.) If you have text files to read in, then you can use the INFILE and INPUT statements in a very simple way since SAS knows how records are defined.

If your file does not adhere to these conventions, then the file is called a "binary" file. Typically, these files do not have the usual record separators, and they may use any binary codes, including unprintable control characters. If you want to read in a binary file, you will have to specify RECFM=U on the INFILE statement and you will need to use the < feature on the INPUT statement to specify the length of each record.

Output files can also be binary, using the RECFM=U option on the FILE statement. The difference between binary and text files on output is that the PUT statement routine does not put the record separator characters on the end of each record written.

Treating a file as binary does allow one to have direct access to a file position by byte-address, using the > feature of the INPUT or PUT statement.

Inputting Data

INFILE Statement

   INFILE *operand options*;

The INFILE statement opens a file for input or, if the file is already open, makes it the current input file so that subsequent INPUT statements read from the file. The INFILE statement *operand* is either a predefined filename or a quoted string or character expression referring to the file path. See **File Naming** earlier in this chapter for further information.

   The *options* available for the INFILE statement are described below:

RECFM=U

   specifies that the file is to be read in as a pure binary file rather than as a file with record separator characters. To do this, you must use the < feature to get new records rather than separate input statements or the / operator.

LENGTH=L

   specifies a variable where the length of a record is to be stored as IML reads it in.

LRECL=*operand*

   specifies the size of the buffer to hold the records. The default size, 512, is enough for most applications.

(*overoptions*)

   specify how IML behaves when an input statement tries to read past the end of a record. The default is STOPOVER. The options are

   MISSOVER

      tolerates attempted reading past the end of the record by assigning missing values to all the variables past the end of the record.

   FLOWOVER

      allows the input statement to go to the next record to obtain values for the variables.

   STOPOVER

      treats going past the end of a record as an error condition, triggering an end-of-file condition.

INPUT Statement

   INPUT *items*;

The INPUT statement reads records from a file specified on the previously executed INFILE statement, reading the values into IML variables.

   The INPUT statement is a sequence of positionals and record directives, input variables, and formats. The *items* used in this statement include:

record-directives

   instruct IML to advance to a new record. Valid record-directives are

   /

      instructs IML to advance to the next record.

   > *operand*

      instructs IML so that the next record read starts at the indicated byte position in the file (for RECFM=U files only).

The *operand* is a literal number, a variable name, or an expression in parentheses.

< *operand*

instructs IML to read in the indicated number of bytes as the next record (for RECFM=U files only). The *operand* is a literal number, a variable name, or an expression in parentheses.

positionals

instruct IML to go to the specified column on the record. Valid positionals include:

@ *operand*

instructs IML to go to the indicated column, where *operand* is a literal number, a variable name, or an expression in parentheses. For example @30 means to go to column 30. The operand can also be a character operand when pattern searching is needed (see **Pattern Searching** later in this chapter).

+ *operand*

specifies that IML skip the indicated number of columns. The *operand* is a literal number, a variable name, or an expression in parentheses.

input variable

specifies the variable you want to read into from the current position in the record. The input variable can be followed immediately by an input format specification.

informat

specifies an input format. These are of the form *w.d* or *$w.* for standard numeric and character informats where *w* is the width of the field and *d* is the decimal parameter, if any. An input format can also be a named format of the form *namew.d* where *name* is the name of the format. Also a single $ or & is allowed for list input applications. If the width is unspecified, then the informat uses list input rules to determine the length by searching for a blank (or comma) delimiter. A special format $RECORD. is used for reading in the remainder of the record into one variable.

holding @-sign

when at the end of an INPUT statement, instructs IML to hold the current record so that you can read more from the record with later INPUT statements. Otherwise, IML automatically goes to the next record for the next INPUT statement.

   Record holding is always implied for RECFM=U binary files, as if the INPUT statement always had a trailing @-sign.

Differences with the DATA Step

If you are familiar with the SAS DATA step, you will notice that the following features are supported differently or are not supported:

- The # directive supporting multiple current records is not supported.
- Grouping parentheses are not supported.
- The default format width is taken from record context rather than by a default width.
- Format modifiers such as & and : are not supported.
- The < and > operators are new features supporting binary files.

• List input values are now delimited by commas as well as blanks.

Examples

The following statement

```
INPUT FOOD $12. @15 CALORIES 5.;
```

instructs IML to read FOOD as a character value twelve characters long starting at the beginning of the record, then position to column 15 of the record and read in a numeric value for CALORIES in the next five positions.

Matrix Use

Input variables always result in scalar (1 row by 1 column) values with type and length according to the input format.

Record Size Limit

There is a limit of 512 characters that can be read at a time to form a record. If you have text records longer than that, then you can use the LRECL option of the INFILE statement to allow larger records.

Scanning (List) Input

If you want the input mechanism to scan across blank space for a value, you use the mechanism called *list input* or *scanning input*. This mechanism is used in the following situations:

1. If no input format is specified for a variable, IML scans for a number.
2. If a single $ or & is specified, IML scans for a character value. The & allows single embedded blanks to occur.
3. If a format is given with width unspecified or zero.

When IML looks for a value, it skips past blanks and tab characters. Then it scans for a delimiter to the value. The delimiter is a blank, a comma, or the end of the record. For the & notation, IML looks for two blanks, a comma, or the end of the record.

If the end of a record is encountered before IML finds a value, then the behavior is as described in **Record Overflow** later in this chapter.

Formatted Input

The alternative to scanning (list) input is formatted input. With formatted input, the variable value is obtained from the current cursor position with a width specified as part of the informat. The informat, specified after the variable name, is of the form

$namew.d

where

$	denotes that the informat is for character rather than numeric result.
name	is the name of the informat. If no name is specified, then IML uses standard character or numeric informats.
w	specifies the width of the field; the number of positions to read the value from.

.   separates the *w* and *d* specifications. A period is always part of a format.

d   is the decimal parameter used with the standard numeric informat to provide a decimal scaling.

Below are some examples of informats:

Format Example	Result Type	Format	Width	Decimal
12.	numeric	standard numeric	12	0
12.2	numeric	standard numeric	12	2
IB4.	numeric	integer binary	4	0
HEX6.	numeric	numeric hexadecimal	6	0
HEX.	numeric	numeric hexadecimal	scanned	0
$6.	character	standard character	6	0
$	character	standard character	scanned	0

Position Directives

Position directives specify the position where values are to be read. There are two position directives:

@ *operand*
    instructs IML to go to a specified position in the record.

+ *operand*
    instructs IML to skip a specified number of positions.

The *operand* can be a number, a variable name, or an expression in parentheses.

Example	Meaning
@12	go to column 12
@N	go to the column given by the value of N
@(N−1)	go to the column given by the value of N−1
+5	skip 5
+N	skip N spaces
+(N+1)	skip N+1 spaces

Pattern Searching

You can have the input mechanism search for patterns of text by using the @ positional with a character operand. IML starts searching at the current position, advances until it finds the pattern, and leaves the pointer at the position immediately after the found pattern in the input record. For example, the statement

```
INPUT @ 'NAME=' NAME $;
```

searches for the pattern 'NAME=' and then uses list input to read the value after the found pattern.

If the pattern is not found, then the pointer is left past the end of the record, and the rest of the input statement follows the conventions based on the options MISSOVER, STOPOVER, FLOWOVER described in **Record Overflow** later in this chapter. If you use pattern searching, you usually specify the MISSOVER option so you can control for the occurrences of the pattern not being found.

Notice that the MISSOVER feature allows you to search for a variety of items on the same record, even if some of them are not found. For example, the statements

```
INFILE IN1 MISSOVER;
INPUT @1 @ "NAME=" name $
      @1 @ "ADDR=" addr $
      @1 @ "PHONE=" phone $;
```

are able to read in the addr variable even if "NAME=" is not found (in which case name is unvalued).

The pattern operand can use any characters except for the following:

% $ [ ] { } < > — ? * # @ ^˜ ` (backquote)

Record Directives

Each input statement goes to a new record except for the following special cases:

1. An @-sign at the end of an input statement specifies that the record is to be held for future input statements.
2. Binary files (RECM=U) always hold their records until the < directive.

As discussed in the syntax of the input statement, the / operator instructs the input mechanism to go immediately to the next record. For binary (RECFM=U) files, the < directive is used instead of the /.

Record Overflow

If you try to read in values from positions past the end of a record, then there are three different actions that could be taken depending on the options specified in the INFILE statement that opened the file. If none of the three is specified, then STOPOVER is implied by default. Below are descriptions of the three options:

MISSOVER
When the end of the record is encountered, the input process stops, and all the variables in the rest of the INPUT statement are freed of their values; that is, missing values are assigned to variables that would have been given values had the record been long enough.

FLOWOVER
When IML reaches the end of the record, the system automatically reads in a new record and positions the pointer in the first column of this new record.

STOPOVER
When input tries to go past the end of a record, it results in an error condition, which triggers diagnostic messages and an end-of-file condition.

End-of-File

End-of-file is the condition of trying to read a record when there are no more records to read from the file. The consequences of an end-of-file condition are described below:

- All the variables in the INPUT statement that encountered end-of-file are freed of their values. You can use the NROW or NCOL function to test if this has happened.
- If end-of-file occurs while inside a DO DATA loop, execution is passed to the statement after the END statement in the loop.

For text files, the end of the file is encountered first as the end of the last record. The next time an input is attempted raises the end-of-file condition.

For binary files, the end-of-file can result in the input mechanism returning a record that is shorter than the requested length. In this case IML still attempts to process the record, using the rules described in **Record Overflow** earlier in this chapter.

The DO DATA mechanism provides a convenient mechanism for handling end-of-file. For example,

```
NAME="12345678";
SEX="1";                        /* DEFINE TYPE-LENGTH */
CREATE CLASS VAR{NAME SEX AGE HEIGHT WEIGHT};
INFILE "CLASS.DAT";
DO DATA;
   INPUT NAME $ SEX $ AGE HEIGHT WEIGHT;
   APPEND;
   END;
CLOSE CLASS;
CLOSEFILE "CLASS.DAT";
```

Note that the APPEND statement is not executed if the INPUT statement reads past the end of file since IML escapes the loop immediately when the condition is encountered.

FILE Statement

FILE *operand options*;

The FILE statement opens a file for output or, if the file is already open, makes it the current output file so that subsequent PUT statements write to the file. The FILE statement is similar in syntax and operation to the INFILE statement described above. The FILE statement *operand* is either a predefined filename or a quoted string or character expression referring to the file path. See **File Naming** earlier in this chapter for details on specifying a file name.

The *options* available for the FILE statement are described below:

RECFM=U

specifies that the file is to be written as a pure binary file without record separator characters.

LRECL=*operand*

specifies the size of the buffer to hold the records. The default size is 512 and is enough for most applications.

PUT Statement

PUT *items*;

The PUT statement writes to the file specified on the previously executed INFILE statement, putting the values from IML variables.

The PUT statement is a sequence of positionals and record directives, variables, and formats. Valid *items* include:

record directives

instruct IML to start new records. Valid record directives include:

/

instructs IML to write the current record and begin a new record.

> operand

instructs IML so that the next record written starts at the indicated byte position in the file (for RECFM=U files only). The *operand* is a literal number, a variable name, or an expression in parentheses.

positionals

instruct IML to go to the specified column on the record. Valid positionals include:

@ operand

instructs IML to go to the indicated column where *operand* is a literal number, a variable name, or an expression in parentheses. For example @30 means to go to column 30.

+ operand

specifies that IML skip the indicated number of columns. The operand is a literal number, a variable name, or an expression in parentheses.

put operand

specifies the value you want to put to the current position in the record. The operand can be either a variable name, a literal value, or an expression in parentheses. The put variable can be followed immediately by an output format specification.

format

specifies an output format. These are of the form *w.d* or $*w.* for standard numeric and character formats where *w* is the width of the field and *d* is the decimal parameter, if any. An output format can also be a named format of the form *namew.d* where *name* is the name of the format. If the width is unspecified, then a default width is used.

holding @-sign

when at the end of a PUT statement, instructs IML to hold the current record so that IML can write more to the record with later PUT statements. Otherwise, IML automatically begins the next record for the next PUT statement.

Determination of the record length   The length of an output record is determined by the minimum size needed to hold all the items specified.

Differences with the DATA step   If you are familiar with the SAS DATA step, you will notice that the following features are supported differently or are not supported:

• The # directive supporting multiple current records is not supported.

• Grouping parentheses are not supported.
• The > operator is a new feature supporting binary files.

Example

Quick printing to the output file   The following few statements generate data
that are printed to the output file:

```
FILE PRINT;
DO A=0 TO 6.28 BY .2;
   X=SIN(A);
   P=(X+1)#30;
   PUT ∂1 A 6.4 +P X 8.4;
END;
```

The result is

```
0.0000                              0.0000
0.2000                                 0.1987
0.4000                                    0.3894
0.6000                                       0.5646
0.8000                                          0.7174
1.0000                                             0.8415
1.2000                                                0.9320
1.4000                                                   0.9854
1.6000                                                      0.9996
1.8000                                                      0.9738
2.0000                                                   0.9093
2.2000                                                0.8085
2.4000                                             0.6755
2.6000                                          0.5155
2.8000                                       0.3350
3.0000                                    0.1411
3.2000                                -0.0584
3.4000                             -0.2555
3.6000                          -0.4425
3.8000                       -0.6119
4.0000                    -0.7568
4.2000                 -0.8716
4.4000             -0.9516
4.6000         -0.9937
4.8000        -0.9962
5.0000        -0.9589
5.2000           -0.8835
5.4000              -0.7728
5.6000                 -0.6313
5.8000                    -0.4646
6.0000                       -0.2794
6.2000                          -0.0831
```

CLOSEFILE Statement

CLOSEFILE *operands*... ;

Use this command to close files opened by INFILE or FILE statements. The *operand* is a filename, a filepath in quotes, or an expression in parentheses. Use the same operand that you used to open the file.

To list out the open files, use the statement

```
SHOW FILES;
```

See **File Naming** earlier in this chapter for more information.

SAS/IML™
Display Features

You can use IML to create windows on your display for full-screen data entry or menuing. The following two statements serve this feature:

    WINDOW   defines a window, its fields, and attributes.

    DISPLAY   displays a window and awaits data entry.

These statements are similar in form and function to the corresponding statements in the DATA step. The specification of fields in the WINDOW or DISPLAY statements is similar to the specifications used in the INPUT and PUT statements. You can write applications using these statements that behave similarly to other full-screen facilities in the SAS System such as AF and FSEDIT. However, the facility in IML is more programmable.

Introductory Example

Suppose your IML application is a data entry system for a mailing list. You want to create a data set called MAILLIST by prompting the user with a window that displays all the entry fields. You want the data entry window to look like this:

```
+--MAILLIST----------------------------------------------+
| Command==>                                             |
|                                                        |
|                                                        |
| NAME:                                                  |
| ADDRESS:                                               |
| CITY:                          STATE:     ZIP:         |
| PHONE:                                                 |
|                                                        |
```

You can generate this window by using WINDOW and DISPLAY statements:

```
WINDOW MAILLIST CMNDLINE=CMND MSGLINE=MSG
     GROUP=ADDR
       #2 " NAME:  "   NAME
       #3 " ADDRESS:" ADDR
       #4 " CITY:  "   CITY  +2 "STATE: " STATE +2 "ZIP: " ZIP
       #5 " PHONE: "  PHONE;
DISPLAY MAILLIST.ADDR;
```

The WINDOW statement creates a window called MAILLIST with a group of
fields (called ADDR) presenting the data fields to enter. The program can send
messages on the window by setting the MSGLINE variable MSG to a value. The
program obtains the commands entered by the user through the CMNDLINE variable CMND.

The whole system can be implemented with the following code:

```
/*---ROUTINE TO INITIALIZE THE VARIABLES---*/
START INITVARS;
   NAME="                          ";
   ADDR="                          ";
   CITY="            "; STATE="  "; ZIP="      ";
   PHONE="                     ";
FINISH;

/*---ROUTINE TO COLLECT ADDRESSES---*/
START MAILGET;

   /*---DEFINE THE WINDOW---*/
   WINDOW MAILLIST CMNDLINE=CMND MSGLINE=MSG
        GROUP=ADDR
          #2 " NAME:  "   NAME
          #3 " ADDRESS:" ADDR
          #4 " CITY:  "   CITY  +2 "STATE: " STATE +2 "ZIP: " ZIP
          #5 " PHONE: "  PHONE;

   /*---GET NEW ADDRESSES UNTIL THE USER COMMANDS EXIT---*/
   DO UNTIL(CMND="EXIT");
      RUN INITVARS; MSG=" ";
      /*---LOOP UNTIL USER TYPES SUBMIT OR EXIT---*/
      DO UNTIL(CMND="SUBMIT" | CMND="EXIT");
         DISPLAY MAILLIST.ADDR;
         MSG="ENTER SUBMIT TO APPEND OBSERVATION, EXIT TO EXIT";
         END;
```

```
            IF CMND="SUBMIT" THEN APPEND;
            END;

        WINDOW CLOSE=MAILLIST;
    FINISH;

    RUN INITVARS;
    CREATE MAILLIST VAR{NAME ADDR CITY STATE ZIP PHONE};
    RUN MAILGET;
    CLOSE MAILLIST;
```

You can enter data into the fields after each prompt field. After you are finished with the entry, press a key defined as SUBMIT, or type SUBMIT in the command entry field. The data are appended to the data set MAILLIST. When all the data entry is completed, enter EXIT in the command entry field. If you enter anything besides SUBMIT, EXIT, or a valid display manager command in the command field, you are given the message

```
enter SUBMIT to append observation, EXIT to exit
```

on the message line.

The WINDOW Statement

The form of the WINDOW statement is

> **WINDOW** <CLOSE=> *windowname* <*windowoptions...*>
> <GROUP=*groupname fieldspecs... >... ;*

where

windowname

is a one to eight character name for the window. This name is displayed in the upper-left border of the window.

CLOSE=

is an option used only when you want to close the window.

windowoptions

control the size, position, and other attributes of the window. You can change the attributes interactively with window commands such as WGROW, WDEF, WSHRINK, and COLOR. The *windowoptions* are described below:

ROWS=*operand*

determines the starting number of rows of the window. The default is 23 rows, and *operand* is either a literal number, the name of a variable containing the number, or an expression in parentheses yielding the number.

COLUMNS=*operand*

specifies the starting number of columns of the window. The default is 78 columns, and *operand* is either a literal number, a variable name, or an expression in parentheses.

IROW=*operand*

specifies the initial starting row position of the window on the display screen. The default is row 1, and *operand* is either a literal number, a variable name, or an expression in parentheses.

ICOLUMN=*operand*

specifies the initial starting column position of the window on the display screen. The default is column 1, and *operand* is either a literal number, a variable name, or an expression in parentheses.

COLOR=operand

specifies the background color for the window. The default color is BLACK, and *operand* is either a quoted character literal, a name, or an operand. The valid values are: BLACK, GREEN, MAGENTA, RED, CYAN, GRAY, and BLUE.

CMNDLINE=*name*

specifies the name of a variable in which the command line entered by the user is to be stored.

MSGLINE=*operand*

specifies the message to be displayed on the standard message line when the window is made active. The *operand* is almost always the name of a variable, but a character literal can be used.

GROUP=*groupname*

starts a repeating sequence of groups of fields defined for the window. The *groupname* is a one to eight character name used to identify a group of fields on a later DISPLAY statement.

fieldspecs

is a sequence of field specifications made up of positionals, field operands, formats and options. These are described in the following section.

Field Specifications

Both the WINDOW and DISPLAY statements allow field specifications. Field specifications have the following form:

<*positionals...*> *fieldoperand* <*format*> <*fieldoptions...*>

where

positionals

are directives specifying the position on the screen to begin the field. There are four kinds of positionals, any number of which are allowed for each field operand. The positionals include:

operand

specifies the row position; that is, it moves the current position to column 1 of the specified line. The *operand* is either a number, a name, or an expression in parentheses.

/

instructs IML to go to column 1 of the next row.

@ *operand*

specifies the column position. The *operand* is either a number, a name, or an expression in parentheses. The @directive should come after the # position, if # is specified.

+ *operand*

is instructs IML to skip columns. The *operand* is either a number, a name, or an expression in parentheses.

fieldoperand

specifies what is to go in the field. It is either a character literal in quotes or the name of a variable.

format

is the format used for display, the value, and also the informat applied to entered values. If no format is specified, the standard numeric or character format is used.

fieldoptions

specify the attributes of the field as follows:

PROTECT=YES
P=YES

specifies that the field is protected; that is, you cannot enter values in the field. If the field operand is a literal, it is already protected.

COLOR=*operand*

specifies the color of the field. The default color is BLUE. The *operand* is a literal character value in quotes, a variable name, or an expression in parentheses. The colors available are: WHITE, BLACK, GREEN, MAGENTA, RED, YELLOW, CYAN, GRAY, and BLUE. Note that the color specification is different from that of the corresponding DATA step value because it is an operand rather than a name without quote marks.

The DISPLAY Statement

After a WINDOW statement has opened the window, use a DISPLAY statement to display the fields in the window.

The DISPLAY statement specifies a list of groups to be displayed. Each group is separated from the next by a comma. The form of the DISPLAY statement is

DISPLAY <*groupspec groupoptions... >,... ;*

where

groupspec

is the specification of a group, either a compound name of the form *windowname.groupname* or a *windowname* followed by a group defined by fields and enclosed in parentheses. For example,

windowname.groupname

or

windowname (fieldspecs...)

where *fieldspecs* is as defined above for the WINDOW statement.

groupoptions

allow you to specify the following options:

NOINPUT

requests that the group be displayed with all the fields protected so that no data entry can be done.

REPEAT

> specifies that the group be repeated for each element of the matrices specified as *fieldoperands*. See **Repeating Fields** below.

BELL

> rings the bell, sounds the alarm, or beeps the speaker at your workstation when the window is displayed.

Details about Windows

Number and position of windows   You can have any number of windows. They can overlap each other or be disjoint. Each window behaves independently from the others. You can specify the starting size, position, and color of the window when you create it. Each window responds to display manager commands so that it can be moved, sized, popped, or changed in color dynamically by the user.

Display surface   A window is really a viewport into a display surface. The display surface can be larger or smaller than the window. If the display surface is larger than the window, you can use scrolling commands to move the surface under the window (or equivalently, move the window over the display surface). The scrolling commands are described below:

RIGHT *n*   scrolls right.

LEFT *n*   scrolls left.

FORWARD *n*   scrolls forward (down).

BACKWARD *n*   scrolls backward (up).

TOP   scrolls to the top of the display surface.

BOTTOM   scrolls to the bottom of the display surface.

The argument *n* is an optional numeric argument to indicate the number of positions to scroll. The default number is 5.

Only one IML window is active at a time. You can move, zoom, enlarge, shrink, and recolor inactive windows, but you cannot scroll or enter data.

Each display surface starts with the same standard lines: first a command line for entering commands, then a message line for displaying messages (such as error messages).

The rest of the display surface is up to you to design. You can put fields in any positive row and column position of the display surface even if it is off the displayed viewport.

Where to define fields   In IML, there is a choice of whether to specify your fields in the WINDOW statement, the DISPLAY statement, or both. Specifying field groups in the WINDOW statement saves work if you access the window from many different DISPLAY statements. Specifying field groups in the DISPLAY statement provides slightly more flexibility.

Groups of fields   All fields must be part of field groups. The group is just a mechanism to treat a group of fields together as a unit in the DISPLAY statement. There are no rules about the field positions of different groups except that **active fields must not overlap.**   Overlapping is acceptable among fields as long as they are not simultaneously active. The active ones are the ones that are specified together in the current DISPLAY statement.

Groups specified in the WINDOW statement are given names. Groups specified in the DISPLAY statement are just put in parentheses and are not named.

Field attributes There are two type of fields you can define: protected fields are for constants on the screen, and unprotected fields accept data entry. If the field consists of a character string in quotes, it is protected. If the field is a variable name, it is not protected unless you specify PROTECT=YES as a field option. If you want all fields protected, you can give the NOINPUT group option in the DISPLAY statement.

Display execution When you execute a DISPLAY statement, the system displays the window with all current values of the variables. You can then enter data into the unprotected fields. All the basic editing keys (cursor controls, delete, end, insert, and so forth) work, as well as display manager commands to scroll or otherwise manage the window. Control does not return to the IML code until you enter a command on the command line that is not recognized as a display manager command. Typically, a SUBMIT command is used since most users define a function key for this often-used command. Before control is returned to the user, IML moves all modified field values from the screen back into IML variables, using standard or specified informat routines. If you have specified the *CMNDLINE=var* option in the WINDOW statement, the current command line is passed back to the specified IML variable.

The window remains visible with the last values entered until the next DISPLAY statement or until the window is closed by a WINDOW CLOSE= statement.

Only one window is active at a time. Every window may be subject to display manager commands, but only the window specified in the currently executing DISPLAY statement transfers data to IML.

Each window display is composed dynamically every time it is displayed. If you position fields by variables, you can make them move to different parts of the screen by simply programming the values of the variables.

The DISPLAY statement even allows general expressions in parentheses as positional or field operands. The WINDOW statement only allows literal constants or variable names as operands. If a field operand is an expression in parentheses, then it is always a protected field. You cannot use the statement

```
DISPLAY W((LOG(X)));
```

and expect it to return the inverse of the log function of the data entered.

Field formatting and inputting The length of a field on the screen is specified in the format after the field operand, if you give one. If a format is not given, IML uses standard character or numeric formats and informats. Numeric informats allow scientific notation and missing values (a dot). The default length for character variables is the size of the variable element. The default size for numeric fields is as given with the IML option FW= (see the **RESET Statement** in the "SAS/IML Language Reference" chapter). If you specify a named format (such as DATE7.), IML attempts to use it for both the output format and input informat. If IML cannot find an input format of that name, it uses the standard informats.

Display-only window If a window consists of only protected fields, it is merely displayed; that is, it does not wait for user input. These display-only windows can be displayed very rapidly (simple displays on a PC/AT can repeat about ten times per second). This is rapid enough for rough animation.

Opening windows The WINDOW statement, like almost all statements in IML, is executable. When a WINDOW statement is executed, it checks to see if the specific window has already been opened. If not, then it opens it; otherwise, it does nothing.

Closing windows   To close a window, use the statement

```
WINDOW CLOSE=windowname;
```

Repeating Fields

If you specify an operand for a field that is a multi-element matrix, the routines deal with the first value of the matrix. However, there is a special REPEAT group option that allows you to display and retrieve values from all the elements of a matrix. If REPEAT is specified, IML determines the maximum number of elements of any field operand matrix, and then it repeats the group that number of times. If any field operand has fewer elements, the last element is repeated the required number of times (the last one becomes the data entered). Be sure to write your specifications so that the fields do not overlap. If the fields overlap, an error message results. Though the fields must be matrices, the positional operands are never treated as matrices.

The REPEAT feature can come in very handy in situations where you want to menu a list of items. For example, suppose you were building a restaurant charging system and you had stored the menu items and prices in the matrices ITEM and PRICE, and you want to obtain the quantity ordered in a matrix called AMOUNT:

```
ITEM={ "Hamburger", "Hot Dog", "Salad Bar", "Milk" };
PRICE={1.10 .90 1.95 .45};
AMOUNT= REPEAT(0,NROW(ITEM),1);
WINDOW MENU
   GROUP=TOP
      #1 a2 "Item"    a44 "Price"    a54 "Amount"
   GROUP=LIST
      /  a2 ITEM $10. a44 PRICE 6.2 a54 AMOUNT 4.
   ;

DISPLAY MENU.TOP, MENU.LIST REPEAT;
```

Example

The following example illustrates the following features:

- multiple windows
- repeat feature
- command and message line usage
- large display surface needing scrolling
- linking windows to data set transactions.

This example uses two windows, FIND and ED. The FIND window instructs you to enter a name. Then a data set is searched for all the names starting with the entered value. If no observations are found, you receive the following message:

```
Not found, enter request
```

If one or more observations are found, then they are displayed in the ED window. You can then edit all the fields. You need to use the scrolling commands to view the entire display surface if several observations are found. If you enter the SUBMIT command, the data are updated in place in the data set. Otherwise, the message displayed is

```
Not Replaced, enter request
```

If you enter a blank field for the request, you are advised that 'exit' is the key word needed to exit the system.

```
START FINDEDIT;
    WINDOW ED   ROWS=10 COLUMNS=40 ICOLUMN=40 CMNDLINE=C;
    WINDOW FIND ROWS=5  COLUMNS=35 ICOLUMN=1  MSGLINE=MSG;
    EDIT USER.CLASS;
    DISPLAY ED ( "Enter a name in the FIND window, and this"
                / "window will display the observations "
                / "starting with that name. Then you can"
                / "edit them and enter the submit command"
                / "to replace them in the data set. Enter cancel"
                / "to not replace the values in the data set."
                /
                / "Enter exit as a name to exit the program."   );

    DO WHILE(1);
       MSG='    ';
    AGAIN:
       NAME="           ";
       DISPLAY FIND ("Search for name: " NAME);

       IF NAME=" "     THEN DO;
          MSG='Enter exit to end';
          GOTO AGAIN;
          END;
       IF NAME="exit"  THEN GOTO X;
          IF NAME="PAUSE" THEN DO;
          PAUSE;
          MSG='Enter again';
          GOTO AGAIN;
          END;

       FIND ALL WHERE(NAME=:NAME) INTO P;
       IF NROW(P)=0 THEN DO;
          MSG='Not found, enter request';
          GOTO AGAIN;
          END;

       READ POINT P;
       DISPLAY ED (//" name: " NAME
                    "  sex: " SEX
                    "  age: " AGE
                   /" height: " HEIGHT
                    "  weight: " WEIGHT ) REPEAT;
       IF C='submit' THEN DO;
          MSG="replaced, enter request";
```

```
            REPLACE POINT P;
            END;
        ELSE DO;
            MSG='Not Replaced, enter request';
            END;
        END;


    X:
    DISPLAY FIND ("Closing Data Set and Exiting");
    CLOSE USER.CLASS;
    WINDOW CLOSE=ED;
    WINDOW CLOSE=FIND;
FINISH;

RUN FINDEDIT;
```

## Chapter 13

Detail Notes

Workspace Storage
Accuracy
Error Diagnostics
Principles of Operation
Operation-level Execution

Workspace Storage

The IML procedure stores matrices in a workspace. To find the size of the work-space and the amount taken up by matrices, use the command:

    SHOW SPACE;

Each active matrix needs $16 + nrow \times ncol \times nsize$ bytes where *nrow* is the number of rows in the matrix, *ncol* is the number of columns, and *nsize* is the length of each element. Numeric elements use 8 bytes each. Many matrix operations need additional storage to perform the computations.

Each time a new matrix is created or replaced, it allocates new memory in the workspace. When the memory is used up, IML recovers unused memory by moving all matrices toward the front of the workspace. This is called a workspace compress. If you find your computer responding slowly, you may be compressing too often and need to allocate a larger workspace.

If you receive an error message saying that not enough space is available, then you may need to restart your IML session with a larger workspace.

The workspace can be specified only at invocation time on the PROC IML statement:

    PROC IML WORKSIZE=nn;

where *nn* is the size of the workspace in K (1024 byte) units.

If you are unable to increase the workspace, try

- freeing intermediate results when they are no longer needed by using the FREE statement.
- using the STORE command to store matrices in IML library data sets and then freeing them until you need to LOAD them later.
- replanning the work to use smaller matrices.

Accuracy

In the IML procedure, all numbers are stored and all arithmetic is done in double precision. The algorithms used are generally very accurate numerically. However, when many operations are performed or when the matrices are ill-conditioned, matrix operations should be used in a numerically responsible way.

Error Diagnostics

When an error occurs, several lines of messages are printed. The error description, the operation being performed, and the line and column of the source for that operation are printed. The names of the operation's arguments are also printed. Matrix names beginning with '#' may appear; these are temporary names assigned by the IML procedure.

When an error occurs, the operation is not completed, and nothing is assigned to the result.

The most common errors are

- not enough workspace (see **Workspace Storage** above)
- referencing a matrix that has not been set to a value
- indexing error; trying to refer to a row or column not present in the matrix
- matrix arguments not conformable; for example, multiplying two matrices together that do not conform or using a function that requires a special scalar or vector argument
- referencing a matrix that is not square (INV, DET, SOLVE, and so forth)
- referencing a matrix that is not symmetric (EIGEN and so forth)
- referencing a matrix that is singular (INV and SOLVE)
- referencing a matrix that is not positive definite or positive semidefinite (HALF and SWEEP).

These errors result from the actual dimensions or values of matrices and are caught only after a statement has begun to execute. Other errors, such as incorrect number of arguments, unbalanced parentheses, and so forth, are syntactical errors and prevent the statement from executing.

Efficiency

The IML language is an interpretive language executor that can be characterized as:

- inexpensive to compile
- expensive for number of operations executed
- inexpensive within each operation.

Users should try to substitute matrix operations for iterative loops. There is a high overhead involved in executing each instruction; however, within the instruction IML runs very efficiently.

Consider four methods of summing the elements of a matrix:

```
1)  S=0;
    DO I=1 TO M;
        DO J=1 TO N;
            S=S+X(I,J);
            END;
        END;
2)  S=J(1,M)*X*J(N,1);
3)  S=X(+,+);
4)  S=SUM(X);
```

Method 1 is very expensive, method 2 is much less expensive, method 3 is less expensive yet, and method 4 is the least expensive.

For some programs that can be written with a few powerful matrix statements, IML can execute even faster than FORTRAN because

- IML has less to compile and compiles faster.
- IML performs efficient indexing of matrices inside the operation.

The greatest advantage of using IML, however, is to reduce human programming labor.

Principles of Operation

This section presents various technical details on the operation of IML software. Statements in IML go through three phases:

1. **Parsing Phase** includes text acquisition, word scanning, recognition, syntactical analysis, and enqueuing on the statement queue. This is performed immediately as IML reads the statements.
2. **Resolution Phase** includes symbol resolution, label and transfer resolution, and function and call resolution. Symbol resolution connects the symbolic names in the statement with their descriptors in the symbol table. New symbols can be added or old ones recognized. Label and transfer resolution connects statements and references affecting the flow of control. This connects LINK and GOTO statements with labels; it connects IF with THEN and ELSE classes; it connects DO with END. Function-call resolution identifies functions and call routines and loads them if necessary. Each reference is checked with respect to the number of arguments allowed. Resolution phase begins after the RUN statement is entered.
3. **Execution Phase** is when the statements are interpreted and executed. There are two levels of execution: statement and operation. Operation-level execution involves the evaluation of expressions within a statement.

Operation-level Execution

Operations are executed from a chain of operation elements created at parse-time and resolved later. For each operation the interpreter:

1. prints a record of the operation if the flow option is on.
2. looks at the operands to make sure they have values. Only certain special operators are allowed to tolerate operands that have not been set to a value. The interpreter checks if any argument has character values.
3. inspects the opcode and gives control to the appropriate execution routine. A separate set of routines is invoked for character values.
4. checks the operands to make sure they are valid for the operation. Then the routine allocates the result matrix and any extra workspace needed for intermediate calculations. Then the work is performed. Extra workspace is freed. A return code notifies IML if the operation was successful. If unsuccessful, it identifies the problem. Control is passed back to the interpreter.
5. checks the return code. If the return code is nonzero, diagnostic routines are called to explain the problem to the user.
6. associates the results with the result arguments in the symbol table. By keeping results out of the symbol table until this time, the operation does not destroy the previous value of the symbol if an error has occurred.
7. prints the result if the PRINT or PRINTALL option is on. The PRINTALL option prints temporary intermediate results as well as end results.
8. moves to the next operation.

Workspace Memory

When IML is invoked, it allocates a portion of the available memory for a workspace. The remaining memory is left unallocated for use by loading modules and their work areas. The workspace is managed by IML in two areas. The area for symbolics is allocated from the top of the workspace and is used by the parser/resolver to assemble control elements such as compiled statements, symbol table elements, and so forth. The area for data values is allocated from the bottom up. Matrix values are stored here. When a matrix value is freed, the area is marked unused so that it can be reclaimed later. As data values get created and freed and symbolic space used, the two areas meet, and IML is out of space. At that time, the memory management routines commence to compress the data value area, moving the matrix values down to lower addresses, compressing out the unused space so that new space becomes available in the middle.

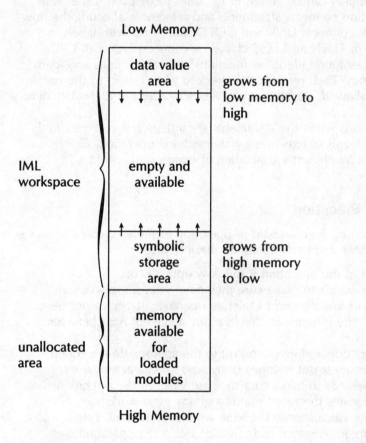

Figure 13.1   SAS/IML Workspace Memory

PART III: EXTENDED EXAMPLES

Applications: Statistical Examples

Applications: Statistical Examples

IML linear operators perform many high-level operations commonly needed in applying linear algebra techniques to data analysis. The similarity of IML notation and matrix algebra notation makes translation from algorithm to program a straightforward task. The examples in this chapter show a variety of matrix operators at work.

Example 1: Correlation

This example computes correlation estimates and standardizes values for a set of data.

```
/*-----CORRELATION-----*/
START CORR;
  N=NROW(X);                      /* DIMENSION OF X */
  SUM=X[+,];                      /* COLUMN SUMS BY REDUCING ROWS */
  XPX=X ` *X-SUM ` *SUM/N;     /* CROSSPRODUCTS CORRECTED FOR MEAN*/
  S=DIAG(1/SQRT(VECDIAG(XPX)));  /* SCALING MATRIX*/
  CORR=S*XPX*S;                   /* CORRELATION MATRIX*/
  PRINT "Correlation Matrix",,CORR[ROWNAME=NM COLNAME=NM];
FINISH;


/*-----STANDARDIZATION-----*/
START STD;
  MEAN=X[+,]/N;                   /* MEANS FOR COLUMNS          */
  X=X-REPEAT(MEAN,N,1);           /* CENTER X TO MEAN ZERO      */
  SS=X[##,];                      /* SUM OF SQUARES FOR COLUMNS */
  STD=SQRT(SS/(N-1));             /* STANDARD DEVIATION ESTIMATE*/
  X=X*DIAG(1/STD);                /* SCALING TO STD DEV 1       */
  PRINT ,"Standardized Data",,X[COLNAME=NM];
FINISH;
```

```
/*-----SAMPLE RUN-----*/
X = { 1    2    3,
      3    2    1,
      4    2    1,
      0    4    1,
     24    1    0,
      1    3    8};
NM={AGE WEIGHT HEIGHT};
RUN CORR;
RUN STD;
```

The results are printed below:

Correlation Matrix

CORR	AGE	WEIGHT	HEIGHT
AGE	1	-.717102	-.436558
WEIGHT	-.717102	1	.3508232
HEIGHT	-.436558	.3508232	1

Standardized Data

X	AGE	WEIGHT	HEIGHT
	-.490116	-.322749	.2264554
	-.272287	-.322749	-.452911
	-.163372	-.322749	-.452911
	-.59903	1.613743	-.452911
	2.014921	-1.29099	-.792594
	-.490116	.6454972	1.924871

Example 2: Newton's Method for Solving Nonlinear Systems of Equations

This example solves a nonlinear system by Newton's method. Let the nonlinear system be represented by

$$F(x)=0$$

where x is a vector and F is a vector-valued, possibly nonlinear function.

In order to find x such that F goes to zero, an initial estimate x_0 is chosen, and Newton's iterative method for converging to the solution is used

$$x_{n+1}=x_n-J^{-1}(x_n)F(x_n)$$

where $J(x)$ is the Jacobian matrix of partial derivatives of F with respect to x.

For optimization problems, the same method is used where $F(x)$ is the gradient of the objective function and $J(x)$ becomes the Hessian (Newton-Raphson).

In this example, the system to be solved is

$$x_1 + x_2 - x_1 * x_2 + 2 = 0$$

$$x_1 * \exp(-x_2) - 1 = 0 \quad .$$

The code is organized into several modules:

```
/*------ NEWTON'S METHOD TO SOLVE A NONLINEAR FUNCTION --------*/
/* THE USER MUST SUPPLY INITIAL VALUES, AND THE FUN AND DERIV  */
/* FUNCTIONS.                                                  */
/* ON ENTRY: FUN EVALUATES THE FUNCTION F IN TERMS OF X        */
/*           INITIAL VALUES ARE GIVEN TO X                     */
/*           DERIV EVALUATES JACOBIAN J                        */
/*           TUNING VARIABLES: CONVERGE, MAXITER.              */
/* ON EXIT:  SOLUTION IN X, FUNCTION VALUE IN F CLOSE TO ZERO  */
/*           ITER HAS NUMBER OF ITERATIONS.                    */
/*------------------------------------------------------------*/
START NEWTON;
  RUN FUN;                      /* EVALUATE FUNCTION AT STARTING VALUES */
  DO ITER=1 TO MAXITER          /* ITERATE UNTIL MAXITER ITERATIONS */
     WHILE(MAX(ABS(F))>CONVERGE); /* OR CONVERGENCE          */
     RUN DERIV;                 /* EVALUATE DERIVATIVES IN J      */
     DELTA=-SOLVE(J,F);         /* SOLVE FOR CORRECTION VECTOR    */
     X=X+DELTA;                 /* THE NEW APPROXIMATION          */
     RUN FUN;                   /* EVALUATE THE FUNCTION          */
     END;
FINISH;

MAXITER=15;                     /* DEFAULT MAXIMUM ITERATIONS    */
CONVERGE=.000001;               /* DEFAULT CONVERGENCE CRITERION */


/*---USER-SUPPLIED FUNCTION EVALUATION---*/
START FUN;
  X1=X[1]; X2=X[2]; /* EXTRACT THE VALUES */
  F= (X1+X2-X1*X2+2)//
     (X1*EXP(-X2)-1);         /* EVAULATE THE FUNCTION */
FINISH;

/*---USER-SUPPLIED DERIVATIVES OF THE FUNCTION---*/
START DERIV;
  J=(    (1-X2)||(1-X1)      )//
    ( EXP(-X2)||(-X1*EXP(-X2))); /* EVALUATE JACOBIAN */
FINISH;

DO;
   PRINT "Solving the system:  X1+X2-X1*X2+2=0,  X1*EXP(-X2)-1=0" ,;
   X={.1, -2};              /* STARTING VALUES */
   RUN NEWTON;
   PRINT X F;
   END;
```

The results are printed below:

```
Solving the system:  X1+X2-X1*X2+2=0,  X1*EXP(-X2)-1=0


                   X          F
            .0977731      .5e-8
           -2.325106      .6e-7
```

Example 3: Regression

This example shows a regression module that calculates statistics not calculated by previous examples:

```
/*--------REGRESSION ROUTINE------------*/
/* GIVEN X, AND Y, THIS FITS Y = X B + E */
/* BY LEAST SQUARES.                     */

START REG;
  N=NROW(X);                     /* NUMBER OF OBSERVATIONS  */
  K=NCOL(X);                     /* NUMBER OF VARIABLES     */
  XPX=X`*X;                      /* CROSS-PRODUCTS          */
  XPY=X`*Y;
  XPXI=INV(XPX);                 /* INVERSE CROSSPRODUCTS   */
  B=XPXI*XPY;                    /* PARAMETER ESTIMATES     */

  YHAT=X*B;                      /* PREDICTED VALUES        */
  RESID=Y-YHAT;                  /* RESIDUALS               */
  SSE=RESID`*RESID;              /* SUM OF SQUARED ERRORS   */
  DFE=N-K;                       /* DEGREES OF FREEDOM ERROR */
  MSE=SSE/DFE;                   /* MEAN SQUARED ERROR      */
  RMSE=SQRT(MSE);                /* ROOT MEAN SQUARED ERROR */

  COVB=XPXI#MSE;                 /* COVARIANCE OF ESTIMATES */
  STDB=SQRT(VECDIAG(COVB));      /* STANDARD ERRORS         */
  T=B/STDB;                      /* TTEST FOR ESTIMATES=0   */
  PROBT=1-PROBF(T#T,1,DFE);      /* SIGNIFICANCE PROBABILITY */
  PRINT NAME B STDB T PROBT;
  S=DIAG(1/STDB);
  CORRB=S*COVB*S;                /* CORRELATION OF ESTIMATES */
  PRINT ,"Covariance of Estimates",  COVB[R=NAME C=NAME],
         "Correlation of Estimates",CORRB[R=NAME C=NAME];

  IF NROW(TVAL)=0 THEN RETURN;/* IS A T-VALUE SPECIFIED?  */
  PROJX=X*XPXI*X`;               /* HAT MATRIX              */
  VRESID=(I(N)-PROJX)*MSE;       /* COVARIANCE OF RESIDUALS */
  VPRED =PROJX#MSE;              /* COVARIANCE OF PREDICTED VALUES */
  H=VECDIAG(PROJX);              /* HAT LEVERAGE VALUES     */
  LOWERM=YHAT-TVAL#SQRT(H*MSE);     /* LOWER CONFIDENCE LIMIT FOR MEAn */
  UPPERM=YHAT+TVAL#SQRT(H*MSE);    /* UPPER */
  LOWER =YHAT-TVAL#SQRT(H*MSE+MSE); /* LOWER CONFIDENCE LIMIT FOR INDiv */
  UPPER =YHAT+TVAL#SQRT(H*MSE+MSE); /* UPPER */
  PRINT ,,"Predicted Values, Residuals, and Limits" ,,
         Y YHAT RESID H LOWERM UPPERM LOWER UPPER;
FINISH;
```

```
/*---ROUTINE TO TEST A LINEAR COMBINATION OF THE ESTIMATES---*/
/* GIVEN L, THIS ROUTINE TESTS HYPOTHESIS THAT L B = 0.        */

START TEST;
  DFN=NROW(L);
  LB=L*B;
  VLB=L*XPXI*L ` ;
  Q=LB ` *INV(VLB)*LB /DFN;
  F=Q/MSE;
  PROB=1-PROBF(F,DFN,DFE);
  PRINT ,F DFN DFE PROB;
FINISH;




/*---RUN IT ON POPULATION OF U.S. FOR DECADES BEGINNING 1790---*/

    X= { 1  1  1,
         1  2  4,
         1  3  9,
         1  4 16,
         1  5 25,
         1  6 36,
         1  7 49,
         1  8 64 };

    Y= {3.929,5.308,7.239,9.638,12.866,17.069,23.191,31.443};

    NAME={"Intercept", "Decade", "Decade**2" };

    TVAL=2.57; /* FOR 5 DF AT .025 LEVEL TO GET 95% confidence interval */

    RESET FW=7;

    RUN REG;

DO;
  PRINT ,"TEST Coef for Linear";        L= {0 1 0      } ; RUN TEST;
  PRINT ,"TEST Coef for Linear,Quad"; L= {0 1 0,0 0 1} ; RUN TEST;
  PRINT ,"TEST Linear+Quad = 0";        L= {0 1 1      } ; RUN TEST;
  END;
```

The results are printed below:

NAME	B	STDB	T	PROBT
Intercept	5.06934	.965594	5.24997	.003326
Decade	-1.1099	.4923	-2.2546	.073851
Decade**2	.539637	.053397	10.106	.000163

```
                  Covariance of Estimates

        COVB       Intercept    Decade Decade**2
        Intercept    .932372   -.43625    .042769
        Decade      -.43625     .24236   -.02566
        Decade**2    .042769   -.02566    .002851


                 Correlation of Estimates

        CORRB      Intercept    Decade Decade**2
        Intercept         1    -.91772    .829502
        Decade      -.91772          1   -.97619
        Decade**2    .829502   -.97619          1



            Predicted Values, Residuals, and Limits


     Y    YHAT   RESID       H LOWERM  UPPERM   LOWER   UPPER
 3.929 4.49904 -.57004 .708333 3.00202 5.99606 2.17419 6.82389
 5.308 5.00802 .299982 .279762 4.06721 5.94883 2.99581 7.02023
 7.239 6.59627 .642732 .232143 5.73926 7.45328 4.62185 8.57069
 9.638 9.26379 .374208 .279762 8.32298 10.2046 7.25158  11.276
12.866 13.0106 -.14459 .279762 12.0698 13.9514 10.9984 15.0228
17.069 17.8367 -.76766 .232143 16.9797 18.6937 15.8622 19.8111
23.191  23.742 -.55101 .279762 22.8012 24.6828 21.7298 25.7542
31.443 30.7266 .716375 .708333 29.2296 32.2236 28.4018 33.0515



                  TEST Coef for Linear

            F     DFN     DFE    PROB
      5.08317       1       5 .073851


                TEST Coef for Linear,Quad

            F     DFN     DFE    PROB
      666.511       2       5 .9e-6


                 TEST Linear+Quad = 0

            F     DFN     DFE    PROB
      1.67746       1       5 .251836
```

Example 4: Alpha Factor Analysis

This example shows how an algorithm for computing alpha factor patterns (Kaiser, 1965) is transcribed into IML code.

For later reference you could store the ALPHA subroutine in this code on a source library and include it when needed.

```
/*--------------- ALPHA FACTOR ANALYSIS -----------------*
| REF: KAISER ET AL., 1965 PSYCHOMETRIKA, PP. 12-13      |
|                                                        |
|                                                        |
|    R   CORRELATION MATRIX (N.S.) ALREADY SET UP        |
|    P   NUMBER OF VARIABLES                              |
|    Q   NUMBER OF FACTORS                                |
|    H   COMMUNALITIES                                    |
|    M   EIGENVALUES                                      |
|    E   EIGENVECTORS                                     |
|    F   FACTOR PATTERN                                   |
|    (IQ,H2,HI,G,MM) TEMPORARY USE. FREED UP             |
*--------------------------------------------------------*/


START ALPHA;
  P=NCOL(R); Q=0; H=0;                    /* INITIALIZE          */
  H2=I(P)-DIAG(1/VECDIAG(INV(R)));        /* SMCS                */


  DO WHILE(MAX(ABS(H-H2))>.001);          /* ITERATE UNTIL CONVERGES */
     H=H2; HI=DIAG(SQRT(1/VECDIAG(H)));
     G=HI*(R-I(P))*HI+I(P);
     CALL EIGEN(M,E,G);                   /* GET EIGENVALUES AND VECS */
     IF Q=0 THEN DO; Q=SUM(M>1);          /* NUMBER OF FACTORS   */
        IQ=1:Q; END;                      /* INDEX VECTOR        */
     MM=DIAG(SQRT(M[IQ, ]));              /* COLLAPSE EIGVALS    */
     E=E[ ,IQ];                           /* COLLAPSE EIGVECS    */
     H2=H*DIAG((E*MM) [,##]);             /* NEW COMMUNALITIES   */
     END;


  HI=SQRT(H); H=VECDIAG(H2);
  F=HI*E*MM;                              /* RESULTING PATTERN   */
  FREE IQ H2 HI G MM;                     /* FREE TEMPORARIES    */
FINISH;




     /*----CORRELATION MATRIX FROM HARMON, MODERN FACTOR ANALYSIS,
        2ND EDITION, PAGE 124, "EIGHT PHYSICAL VARIABLES" */
     R={1.000    .846    .805    .859    .473    .398    .301    .382 ,
        .846    1.000    .881    .826    .376    .326    .277    .415 ,
        .805    .881    1.000    .801    .380    .319    .237    .345 ,
        .859    .826    .801    1.000    .436    .329    .327    .365 ,
        .473    .376    .380    .436    1.000    .762    .730    .629 ,
        .398    .326    .319    .329    .762    1.000    .583    .577 ,
        .301    .277    .237    .327    .730    .583    1.000    .539 ,
        .382    .415    .345    .365    .629    .577    .539    1.000};
  NM = {Var1 Var2 Var3 Var4 Var5 Var6 Var7 Var8};

  RUN ALPHA;
  PRINT  ,"EIGENVALUES"   , M;
  PRINT  ,"COMMUNALITIES" , H[ROWNAME=NM];
  PRINT  ,"FACTOR PATTERN", F[ROWNAME=NM];
```

The results are printed below:

```
                        EIGENVALUES

                             M
                         5.937855
                         2.0621956
                          .13901778
                          .08210537
                          .01809701
                         -.0474866
                         -.0914798
                         -.1003044


                        COMMUNALITIES

                    H
                    VAR1  .83812049
                    VAR2  .89057171
                    VAR3  .81893002
                    VAR4   .8067292
                    VAR5  .88021492
                    VAR6  .63919774
                    VAR7  .58215827
                    VAR8  .49981261


                        FACTOR PATTERN

                 F
                 VAR1  .81338598  -.4201473
                 VAR2  .80283626  -.4960097
                 VAR3  .75790868  -.4944739
                 VAR4  .78744612  -.4320391
                 VAR5  .80514386   .48162048
                 VAR6   .6804127   .41980507
                 VAR7  .62062299   .44383033
                 VAR8  .64494194   .28959025
```

Example 5: Categorical Linear Models

This example uses PROC IML to fit a linear model to a function of the response probabilities

$$\mathbf{K} \, log \, \pi = \mathbf{X}\beta + \mathbf{e}$$

where **K** is a matrix that compares each response category to the last. Data were obtained from Kastenbaum and Lamphiear (1959). First, the Grizzle-Starmer-Koch (1969) approach is used to obtain generalized least-squares estimates of β. These form the initial values for the Newton-Raphson solution for the maximum-likelihood estimates. PROC CATMOD can also be used to analyze these binary data (see Cox, 1970).

```
/* CATEGORICAL LINEAR MODELS BY LEAST SQUARES AND MAXIMUM LIKELIHOOD */

START CATLIN;

 /*-----------CATLIN-------------------------*
  | INPUT:                                   |
  |   N   THE S BY P MATRIX OF RESPONSE COUNTS |
  |   X   THE S BY R DESIGN MATRIX            |
  |                                          |
  *------------------------------------------*/


 /*---FIND DIMENSIONS---*/
 S=NROW(N);                    /* NUMBER OF POPULATIONS    */
 R=NCOL(N);                    /* NUMBER OF RESPONSES      */
 Q=R-1;                        /* NUMBER OF FUNCTION VALUES */
 D=NCOL(X);                    /* NUMBER OF DESIGN PARAMETERS*/
 QD=Q*D;                       /* TOTAL NUMBER OF PARAMETERS */

 /*---GET PROBABILITY ESTIMATES---*/
 ROWN=N[,+];                   /* ROW TOTALS*/
 PR=N/(ROWN*REPEAT(1,1,R));    /* PROBABILITY ESTIMATES*/
 P=SHAPE(PR[,1:Q],0,1);        /* CUT AND SHAPED TO VECTOR*/
 PRINT "INITIAL PROBABILITY ESTIMATES" ,PR;

 /*---ESTIMATE BY THE GSK METHOD---*/
 F=LOG(P)-LOG(PR[,R])@REPEAT(1,Q,1); /* FUNCTION OF PROBABILITIES*/
 SI=(DIAG(P)-P*P`)#
    (DIAG(ROWN)@REPEAT(1,Q,Q)); /* INV COVARIANCE OF F*/
 Z=X@I(Q);                     /* EXPANDED DESIGN MATRIX  */
 H=Z`*SI*Z;                    /* CROSSPRODUCTS MATRIX    */
 G=Z`*SI*F;                    /* CROSS WITH F            */
 BETA=SOLVE(H,G);              /* LEAST SQUARES SOLUTION  */
 STDERR=SQRT(VECDIAG(INV(H))); /* STANDARD ERRORS    */

 RUN PROB; PRINT ,"GSK ESTIMATES" , BETA STDERR ,PI;

 /*---ITERATIONS FOR ML SOLUTION---*/
 CRIT=1;

 DO IT=1 TO 8 WHILE(CRIT>.0005);  /* ITERATE UNTIL CONVERGE*/
    SI=(DIAG(PI)-PI*PI`) #
       (DIAG(ROWN)@REPEAT(1,Q,Q));      /* BLOCK DIAGONAL WEIGHTING*/
    G=Z`*(ROWN@REPEAT(1,Q,1)#(P-PI)); /* GRADIENT*/
    H=Z`*SI*Z;                /* HESSIAN*/
    DELTA=SOLVE(H,G);         /* SOLVE FOR CORRECTION*/
    BETA=BETA+DELTA;          /* APPLY THE CORRECTION*/
    RUN PROB;                 /* COMPUTE PROB ESTIMATES*/
    CRIT=MAX(ABS(DELTA));     /* CONVERGENCE CRITERION */
    END;

  STDERR=SQRT(VECDIAG(INV(H))); /* STANDARD ERRORS */
  PRINT , "ML Estimates", BETA STDERR, PI;
  PRINT , "Iterations" IT "Criterion" CRIT;
 FINISH;
```

```
      /*---SUBROUTINE TO COMPUTE NEW PROB ESTIMATES @ PARAMETERS*/
   START PROB;
     LA=EXP(X*SHAPE(BETA,0,Q));
     PI=LA/((1+LA[,+])*REPEAT(1,1,Q));
     PI=SHAPE(PI,0,1);
   FINISH;


   /*---PREPARE FREQUENCY DATA AND DESIGN MATRIX---*/
   N= { 58 11 05,
        75 19 07,
        49 14 10,
        58 17 08,
        33 18 15,
        45 22 10,
        15 13 15,
        39 22 18,
        04 12 17,
        05 15 08};                 /* FREQUENCY COUNTS*/


   X= { 1  1  1  0  0  0,
        1 -1  1  0  0  0,
        1  1  0  1  0  0,
        1 -1  0  1  0  0,
        1  1  0  0  1  0,
        1 -1  0  0  1  0,
        1  1  0  0  0  1,
        1 -1  0  0  0  1,
        1  1 -1 -1 -1 -1,
        1 -1 -1 -1 -1 -1};         /* DESIGN MATRIX*/

   RUN CATLIN;
```

The results are printed below:

INITIAL PROBABILITY ESTIMATES

```
                  PR
        .78378378 .14864865 .06756757
        .74257426 .18811881 .06930693
        .67123288 .19178082 .1369863
        .69879518 .20481928 .09638554
              .5 .27272727 .22727273
        .58441558 .28571429 .12987013
        .34883721 .30232558 .34883721
        .49367089 .27848101 .2278481
        .12121212 .36363636 .51515152
        .17857143 .53571429 .28571429
```

GSK ESTIMATES

BETA	STDERR
.94544289	.12909246
.40032593	.12848673
-.2777766	.11646991
-.2784716	.12559156
1.4146936	.26735097
.47413601	.29494301
.8464701	.23626394
.15260949	.26330513
.19523948	.22144363
.07234891	.2366597
-.5144883	.21719945
-.4008315	.22857787

PI

.74028666
.16744717
.77040575
.17450227
.66248108
.19177435
.70616153
.20470326
.51698097
.26488705
.5697446
.29232776
.39886951
.25890964
.46679241
.30342044
.1320359
.39580194
.16519072
.49587841

ML Estimates

BETA	STDERR
.95335967	.12861787
.40693385	.12845918
-.2790811	.11562221
-.2806993	.12528164
1.4423195	.26693575
.49931231	.29434367
.84115946	.23630893
.14858746	.26351594
.18833833	.22027545
.06673131	.23603098
-.5271627	.21658099
-.4149654	.22996183

```
                                PI
                          .74317586
                          .16731555
                          .77232659
                          .17444207
                          .66272657
                          .19166451
                          .70627663
                          .20492158
                          .51707823
                          .26468572
                          .5697771
                          .29260705
                          .39842053
                          .25766527
                          .46668249
                          .30278979
                          .13232426
                          .3963114
                          .16547498
                          .49720442


                          IT              CRIT
       Iterations          3   Criterion .00040925
```

Example 6: Regression of Subsets of Variables

The following example performs regression with variable selection like some of
the features in the REG procedure. It is a very large program that may not fit in
your machine unless you have a large amount of memory and use the WORKSIZE
option to allocate a large workspace. (It needs a minimum workspace of 45K.)

```
/*-------INITIALIZATION-------------------------------*
| C,CSAVE THE CROSSPRODUCTS MATRIX                     |
| N       NUMBER OF OBSERVATIONS                       |
| K       TOTAL NUMBER OF VARIABLES TO CONSIDER        |
| L       NUMBER OF VARIABLES CURRENTLY IN MODEL       |
| IN      A 0-1 VECTOR OF WHETHER VARIABLE IS IN       |
| B       PRINT COLLECTS RESULTS (L MSE RSQ BETAS )    |
*----------------------------------------------------*/
START INITIAL;
 N=NROW(X); K=NCOL(X); K1=K+1; IK=1:K;
 BNAMES={NPARM MSE RSQUARE} ||VARNAMES;

 /*---CORRECT BY MEAN, ADJUST OUT INTERCEPT PARAMETER---*/
 Y=Y-Y[+,]/N;                    /* CORRECT Y BY MEAN */
 X=X-REPEAT(X[+,]/N,N,1);        /* CORRECT X BY MEAN */
 XPY=X`*Y;                       /* CROSSPRODUCTS     */
 YPY=Y`*Y;
 XPX=X`*X;
 FREE X Y;                       /* NO LONGER NEED THE DATA*/
 CSAVE=(XPX || XPY) //
       (XPY` || YPY);            /* SAVED COPY OF CROSSPRODUCTS*/
FINISH;
```

```
/*-----FORWARD METHOD--------------------------------------------------*/
START FORWARD;
  PRINT / "FORWARD SELECTION METHOD";
  FREE BPRINT;
  C=CSAVE; IN=REPEAT(0,K,1); L=0;        /* NO VARIABLES ARE IN */
  DFE=N-1; MSE=YPY/DFE;
  SPROB=0;

  DO WHILE(SPROB<.15 & L<K);
      INDX=LOC(^IN);                /* WHERE ARE THE VARIABLES NOT IN?*/
      CD=VECDIAG(C)[INDX,];         /* XPX DIAGONALS                  */
      CB=C[INDX,K1];                /* ADJUSTED XPY                   */
      TSQR=CB#CB/(CD#MSE);          /* SQUARES OF T TESTS             */
      IMAX=TSQR[<:>,];              /* LOCATION OF MAXIMUM IN INDX    */
      SPROB=(1-PROBT(SQRT(TSQR[IMAX,]),DFE))*2;
      IF SPROB<.15 THEN DO;         /* IF T-TEST SIGNIFICANT          */
         II=INDX[,IMAX];            /* PICK MOST SIGNIFICANT          */
         RUN SWP;                   /* ROUTINE TO SWEEP               */
         RUN BPR;                   /* ROUTINE TO COLLECT RESULTS     */
         END;
      END;

  PRINT , BPRINT[COLNAME=BNAMES];
FINISH;


/*-----BACKWARD METHOD-------------------------------------------------*/
START BACKWARD;
  PRINT / "BACKWARD ELIMINATION ";
  FREE BPRINT;
  C=CSAVE; IN=REPEAT(0,K,1);
  II=1:K; RUN SWP; RUN BPR;         /* START WITH ALL VARIABLES IN*/
  SPROB=1;

  DO WHILE(SPROB>.15 & L>0);
     INDX=LOC(IN);                  /* WHERE ARE THE VARIABLES IN? */
     CD=VECDIAG(C)[INDX,];          /* XPX DIAGONALS               */
     CB=C[INDX,K1];                 /* BVALUES                     */
     TSQR=CB#CB/(CD#MSE);           /* SQUARES OF T TESTS          */
     IMIN=TSQR[>:<,];               /* LOCATION OF MINIMUM IN INDX */
     SPROB=(1-PROBT(SQRT(TSQR[IMIN,]),DFE))*2;
     IF SPROB>.15 THEN DO;          /* IF T-TEST NONSIGNIFICANT    */
        II=INDX[,IMIN];             /* PICK LEAST SIGNIFICANT       */
        RUN SWP;                    /* ROUTINE TO SWEEP IN VARIABLE*/
        RUN BPR;                    /* ROUTINE TO COLLECT RESULTS  */
        END;
     END;

  PRINT , BPRINT[COLNAME=BNAMES];
FINISH;
```

```
/*-----STEPWISE METHOD------------------------------------------------*/
START STEPWISE;
  PRINT /"STEPWISE METHOD";
  FREE BPRINT;
  C=CSAVE; IN=REPEAT(0,K,1); L=0;
  DFE=N-1; MSE=YPY/DFE;
  SPROB=0;

  DO WHILE(SPROB<.15 & L<K);
      INDX=LOC(^IN);                     /*WHERE ARE THE VARIABLES NOT IN?*/
      NINDX=LOC(IN);                     /* WHERE ARE THE VARIABLES IN?   */
      CD=VECDIAG(C)[INDX,];              /* XPX DIAGONALS                 */
      CB=C[INDX,K1];                     /* ADJUSTED XPY                  */
      TSQR=CB#CB/CD/MSE;                 /* SQUARES OF T TESTS            */
      IMAX=TSQR[<:>,];                   /* LOCATION OF MAXIMUM IN INDX   */
      SPROB=(1-PROBT(SQRT(TSQR[IMAX,]),DFE))*2;
      IF SPROB<.15 THEN DO;              /* IF T-TEST SIGNIFICANT         */
         II=INDX[,IMAX];                 /* FIND INDEX INTO C             */
         RUN SWP;                        /* ROUTINE TO SWEEP              */
         RUN BACKSTEP;                   /* CHECK IF REMOVE ANY TERMS     */
         RUN BPR;                        /* ROUTINE TO COLLECT RESULTS    */
         END;
      END;

  PRINT , BPRINT[COLNAME=BNAMES];
FINISH;


/*----ROUTINE TO BACKWARDS-ELIMINATE FOR STEPWISE--*/
START BACKSTEP;
  IF NROW(NINDX)=0 THEN RETURN;
  BPROB=1;
  DO WHILE(BPROB>.15 & L<K);
      CD=VECDIAG(C)[NINDX,];             /* XPX DIAGONALS        */
      CB=C[NINDX,K1];                    /* BVALUES              */
      TSQR=CB#CB/(CD#MSE);               /* SQUARES OF T TESTS   */
      IMIN=TSQR[>:<,];                   /* LOCATION OF MINIMUM IN NINDX*/
      BPROB=(1-PROBT(SQRT(TSQR[IMIN,]),DFE))*2;
      IF BPROB>.15 THEN DO;
         II=NINDX[,IMIN];
         RUN SWP;
         RUN BPR;
         END;
      END;
FINISH;
```

```
/*-----SEARCH ALL POSSIBLE MODELS------------------------------------------*/
START ALL;
     /*---USE METHOD OF SCHATZOFF ET AL. FOR SEARCH TECHNIQUE-------*/
     BETAK=REPEAT(0,K,K);   /* RECORD ESTIMATES FOR BEST L-PARAM MODEL*/
     MSEK=REPEAT(1E50,K,1);/* RECORD BEST MSE PER # PARMS        */
     RSQK=REPEAT(0,K,1);    /* RECORD BEST RSQUARE                */
     INK=REPEAT(0,K,K);     /* RECORD BEST SET PER # PARMS        */
     LIMIT=2##K-1;          /* NUMBER OF MODELS TO EXAMINE        */

     C=CSAVE; IN=REPEAT(0,K,1);/* START OUT WITH NO VARIABLES IN MODEL   */

     DO KK=1 TO LIMIT;
        RUN ZTRAIL;                 /* FIND WHICH ONE TO SWEEP     */
        RUN SWP;                    /* SWEEP IT IN                 */
       BB=BB//(L||MSE||RSQ||(C[IK,K1]#IN)`);
       IF MSE<MSEK[L,] THEN DO; /* WAS THIS BEST FOR L PARMS? */
           MSEK[L,]=MSE;            /* RECORD MSE                 */
           RSQK[L,]=RSQ;            /* RECORD RSQUARE             */
           INK[,L]=IN;              /* RECORD WHICH PARMS IN MODEL*/
           BETAK[L,]=(C[IK,K1]#IN)`;             /* RECORD ESTIMATES */
           END;
        END;

     PRINT / "ALL POSSIBLE MODELS" " IN SEARCH ORDER",;
     PRINT BB[COLNAME=BNAMES]; FREE BB;
     BPRINT=IK`||MSEK||RSQK||BETAK;
     PRINT , "THE BEST MODEL FOR EACH NUMBER OF PARAMETERS";
     PRINT , BPRINT[COLNAME=BNAMES];

     /*---MALLOWS CP PLOT---*/
     CP=MSEK#(N-IK`-1)/MIN(MSEK)-(N-2#IK`);
     CP=IK`||CP;
     CPNAME={"NPARM" "CP"};
     /*OUTPUT CP OUT=CP COLNAME=CPNAME;*/
FINISH;




/*-----SUBROUTINE TO FIND NUMBER OF TRAILING ZEROS IN BINARY NUMBER---*/
/* ON ENTRY: KK IS THE NUMBER TO EXAMINE                              */
/* ON EXIT:  II HAS THE RESULT                                        */
/*------------------------------------------------------------------*/
START ZTRAIL;
    II=1; ZZ=KK;
    DO WHILE(MOD(ZZ,2)=0); II=II+1; ZZ=ZZ/2; END;
FINISH;
```

```
/*-----SUBROUTINE TO SWEEP IN A PIVOT----------------------------------*/
/* ON ENTRY: II HAS THE POSITION(S) TO PIVOT                           */
/* ON EXIT:  IN, L, DFE, MSE, RSQ RECALCULATED                         */
/*---------------------------------------------------------------------*/
START SWP;
    IF ABS(C[II,II])<1E-9 THEN DO; PRINT , "FAILURE", C; STOP; END;
    C=SWEEP(C,II);
    IN II, =^IN II, ;
    L=SUM(IN); DFE=N-1-L;
    SSE=C[K1,K1];
    MSE=SSE/DFE;
    RSQ=1-SSE/YPY;
FINISH;


/*-----SUBROUTINE TO COLLECT BPRINT RESULTS----------------------------*/
/* ON ENTRY: L,MSE,RSQ, AND C SET UP TO COLLECT                        */
/* ON EXIT:  BPRINT HAS ANOTHER ROW                                    */
/*---------------------------------------------------------------------*/
START BPR;
    BPRINT=BPRINT//(L||MSE||RSQ||(C[IK,K1]#IN) ` );
FINISH;



 /*-------------STEPWISE METHODS--------------------*/
 /* AFTER A RUN TO THE INITIAL ROUTINE, WHICH SETS UP */
 /* THE DATA, FOUR DIFFERENT ROUTINES CAN BE CALLED   */
 /* TO DO FOUR DIFFERENT MODEL-SELECTION METHODS.     */
 /*-------------------------------------------------*/
START SEQ;
  RUN INITIAL;        /* INITIALIZATION             */
  RUN ALL;            /* ALL POSSIBLE MODELS        */
  RUN FORWARD;        /* FOREWARD SELECTION METHOD  */
  RUN BACKWARD;       /* BACKWARD ELIMINATION METHOD*/
  RUN STEPWISE;       /* STEPWISE METHOD            */
FINISH;
```

```
/*----------------------DATA ON PHYSICAL FITNESS--------------------*
| THESE MEASUREMENTS WERE MADE ON MEN INVOLVED IN A PHYSICAL FITNESS |
| COURSE AT N.C.STATE UNIV.  THE VARIABLES ARE AGE(YEARS), WEIGHT(KG),|
| OXYGEN UPTAKE RATE(ML PER KG BODY WEIGHT PER MINUTE), TIME TO RUN  |
| 1.5 MILES(MINUTES), HEART RATE WHILE RESTING, HEART RATE WHILE     |
| RUNNING (SAME TIME OXYGEN RATE MEASURED), AND MAXIMUM HEART RATE   |
| RECORDED WHILE RUNNING. CERTAIN VALUES OF MAXPULSE WERE MODIFIED   |
| FOR CONSISTENCY.         DATA COURTESY DR. A.C. LINNERUD           |
*------------------------------------------------------------------*/

DATA =
   ( 44 89.47  44.609 11.37 62 178 182 ,
     40 75.07  45.313 10.07 62 185 185 ,
     44 85.84  54.297  8.65 45 156 168 ,
     42 68.15  59.571  8.17 40 166 172 ,
     38 89.02  49.874  9.22 55 178 180 ,
     47 77.45  44.811 11.63 58 176 176 ,
     40 75.98  45.681 11.95 70 176 180 ,
     43 81.19  49.091 10.85 64 162 170 ,
     44 81.42  39.442 13.08 63 174 176 ,
     38 81.87  60.055  8.63 48 170 186 ,
     44 73.03  50.541 10.13 45 168 168 ,
     45 87.66  37.388 14.03 56 186 192 ,
     45 66.45  44.754 11.12 51 176 176 ,
     47 79.15  47.273 10.60 47 162 164 ,
     54 83.12  51.855 10.33 50 166 170 ,
     49 81.42  49.156  8.95 44 180 185 ,
     51 69.63  40.836 10.95 57 168 172 ,
     51 77.91  46.672 10.00 48 162 168 ,
     48 91.63  46.774 10.25 48 162 164 ,
     49 73.37  50.388 10.08 67 168 168 ,
     57 73.37  39.407 12.63 58 174 176 ,
     54 79.38  46.080 11.17 62 156 165 ,
     52 76.32  45.441  9.63 48 164 166 ,
     50 70.87  54.625  8.92 48 146 155 ,
     51 67.25  45.118 11.08 48 172 172 ,
     54 91.63  39.203 12.88 44 168 172 ,
     51 73.71  45.790 10.47 59 186 188 ,
     57 59.08  50.545  9.93 49 148 155 ,
     49 76.32  48.673  9.40 56 186 188 ,
     48 61.24  47.920 11.50 52 170 176 ,
     52 82.78  47.467 10.50 53 170 172 );


X=DATA[,{ 1 2 4 5 6 7 }];
Y=DATA[,3];
VARNAMES={AGE WEIGHT RUNTIME RSTPULSE RUNPULSE MAXPULSE};

RESET FW=8 LINESIZE=90;

RUN SEQ;
```

The results are printed below:

ALL POSSIBLE MODELS   IN SEARCH ORDER

BB NPARM	MSE	RSQUARE	AGE	WEIGHT	RUNTIME	RSTPULSE	RUNPULSE	MAXPULSE
1	26.63425	.0927765	-.31136	0	0	0	0	0
2	25.82619	.1506353	-.370416	-.158232	0	0	0	0
1	28.58034	.0264885	0	-.104102	0	0	0	0
2	7.755636	.7449348	0	-.025484	-3.2886	0	0	0
3	7.226318	.7708306	-.173877	-.054437	-3.14039	0	0	0
2	7.168422	.7642469	-.150366	0	-3.20395	0	0	0
1	7.533843	.7433801	0	0	-3.31056	0	0	0
2	7.798261	.743533	0	0	-3.28661	-.009682	0	0
3	7.336089	.7673494	-.167547	0	-3.07925	-.045492	0	0
4	7.366649	.7750328	-.196026	-.059152	-2.9889	-.053255	0	0
3	8.037314	.7451114	0	-.025685	-3.26268	-.010409	0	0
2	24.91487	.1806067	0	-.093049	0	-.274742	0	0
3	20.28031	.3568473	-.446982	-.156472	0	-.321863	0	0
2	21.27632	.3002703	-.388821	0	0	-.322856	0	0
1	24.67582	.1594853	0	0	0	-.279215	0	0
2	23.26003	.2350307	0	0	0	-.206838	-.152617	0
3	16.81799	.4666484	-.523382	0	0	-.225238	-.237688	0
4	16.26146	.5033977	-.563168	-.12697	0	-.229807	-.224602	0
3	23.81815	.2446512	0	-.063813	0	-.208432	-.142789	0
4	7.785151	.7622524	0	-.012313	-3.16759	.0166688	-.074897	0
5	6.213174	.8175561	-.285277	-.051844	-2.70392	-.027109	-.126278	0
4	6.166944	.8116702	-.262126	0	-2.77733	-.019814	-.128741	0
3	7.507972	.7618985	0	0	-3.17665	.0176163	-.076576	0
2	7.254263	.7614238	0	0	-3.14019	0	-.073509	0
3	5.956692	.8110945	-.256398	0	-2.82538	0	-.130909	0
4	6.009033	.8164926	-.276417	-.049323	-2.77237	0	-.129324	0
3	7.510162	.761829	0	-.01315	-3.13261	0	-.071892	0
2	25.333	.1668554	0	-.059868	0	0	-.197971	0
3	18.63184	.4091255	-.544083	-.120495	0	0	-.282478	0
2	18.97378	.3759954	-.506648	0	0	0	-.293816	0
1	24.70817	.1583834	0	0	0	0	-.206799	0
2	21.60626	.2894195	0	0	0	0	-.6818	.5715377
3	18.21725	.4222735	-.421398	0	0	0	-.579662	.3615574
4	17.29877	.4717197	-.452427	-.149436	0	0	-.61723	.4268622
3	21.41763	.3207793	0	-.11815	0	0	-.717449	.6353949
4	6.030105	.815849	0	-.051587	-2.9255	0	-.395293	.3853699
5	5.176338	.8480018	-.219621	-.072302	-2.68252	0	-.373401	.3049078
4	5.343462	.8368181	-.197735	0	-2.76758	0	-.348108	.270513
3	5.991568	.8099884	0	0	-2.97019	0	-.375114	.3542189
4	6.208523	.8104004	0	0	-3.00426	.016412	-.377784	.3539983
5	5.549941	.8370313	-.20154	0	-2.7386	-.012078	-.345624	.2690644
6	5.368247	.8486719	-.226974	-.074177	-2.62865	-.021534	-.369628	.3032171
5	6.263348	.8160828	0	-.050907	-2.95182	.01239	-.397042	.3847928
4	20.11235	.3857969	0	-.1194	0	-.190917	-.645842	.6096323
5	15.1864	.5540659	-.479225	-.1527	0	-.215547	-.530449	.3854238
4	16.29247	.5024508	-.447169	0	0	-.212659	-.493234	.3192669
3	20.37729	.3537718	0	0	0	-.189933	-.610187	.5452359
2	25.11456	.1740393	0	0	0	-.25219	0	-.073642
3	19.2347	.3900068	-.527358	0	0	-.26492	0	-.200243

```
4 18.80875 .4256071 -.558811 -.126038        0 -.270558        0 -.17799
3 25.59719 .1882321        0 -.078736        0 -.255238        0 -.055024
4 8.311496 .7461785        0 -.02053 -3.25232 -.003933        0 -.020639
5 7.19584 .7887011 -.257952 -.04936 -2.86147 -.041206        0 -.081534
4 7.091611 .7834321 -.239284        0 -2.92597 -.033905        0 -.087769
3 8.033673 .7452268        0        0 -3.26805 -.001934        0 -.025261
2 7.746932 .7452211        0        0 -3.27232        0        0 -.025605
3 6.882626 .7817302 -.229232        0 -3.01222        0        0 -.090944
4 7.00018 .7862243 -.244362 -.045249 -2.97011        0        0 -.085854
3 8.00441 .7461549        0 -.02027 -3.26114        0        0 -.021394
2 28.35356 .0675159        0 -.070738        0        0        0 -.121588
3 22.38148 .2902125 -.540763 -.116048        0        0        0 -.24445
2 22.50135 .2599817 -.512102        0        0        0        0 -.263695
1 27.71259 .0560459        0        0        0        0        0 -.137621
```

THE BEST MODEL FOR EACH NUMBER OF PARAMETERS

BPRINT NPARM	MSE	RSQUARE	AGE	WEIGHT	RUNTIME	RSTPULSE	RUNPULSE	MAXPULSE
1	7.533843	.7433801	0	0	-3.31056	0	0	0
2	7.168422	.7642469	-.150366	0	-3.20395	0	0	0
3	5.956692	.8110945	-.256398	0	-2.82538	0	-.130909	0
4	5.343462	.8368181	-.197735	0	-2.76758	0	-.348108	.270513
5	5.176338	.8480018	-.219621	-.072302	-2.68252	0	-.373401	.3049078
6	5.368247	.8486719	-.226974	-.074177	-2.62865	-.021534	-.369628	.3032171

FORWARD SELECTION METHOD

BPRINT NPARM	MSE	RSQUARE	AGE	WEIGHT	RUNTIME	RSTPULSE	RUNPULSE	MAXPULSE
1	7.533843	.7433801	0	0	-3.31056	0	0	0
2	7.168422	.7642469	-.150366	0	-3.20395	0	0	0
3	5.956692	.8110945	-.256398	0	-2.82538	0	-.130909	0
4	5.343462	.8368181	-.197735	0	-2.76758	0	-.348108	.270513

BACKWARD ELIMINATION

BPRINT NPARM	MSE	RSQUARE	AGE	WEIGHT	RUNTIME	RSTPULSE	RUNPULSE	MAXPULSE
6	5.368247	.8486719	-.226974	-.074177	-2.62865	-.021534	-.369628	.3032171
5	5.176338	.8480018	-.219621	-.072302	-2.68252	0	-.373401	.3049078
4	5.343462	.8368181	-.197735	0	-2.76758	0	-.348108	.270513

STEPWISE METHOD

BPRINT NPARM	MSE	RSQUARE	AGE	WEIGHT	RUNTIME	RSTPULSE	RUNPULSE	MAXPULSE
1	7.533843	.7433801	0	0	-3.31056	0	0	0
2	7.168422	.7642469	-.150366	0	-3.20395	0	0	0
3	5.956692	.8110945	-.256398	0	-2.82538	0	-.130909	0
4	5.343462	.8368181	-.197735	0	-2.76758	0	-.348108	.270513

Example 7: Response Surface Methodology

A regression model with a complete quadratic set of regressions across several factors can be processed to yield the estimated critical values that may optimize a response. First, the regression is done for 2 variables according to the model:

$$y = c + b_1 x_1 + b_2 x_2 + a_{11} x_1^2 + a_{12} x_1 x_2 + a_{22} x_2^2 + e \quad .$$

The estimates are then divided into a vector of linear coefficients (estimates) **b** and a matrix of quadratic coefficients **A**. Then the solution for critical values is

$$x = -.5A^{-1}b \quad .$$

```
/*----------QUADRATIC RESPONSE SURFACE REGRESSION---------------*
| THIS MATRIX ROUTINE READS IN THE FACTOR VARIABLES AND THE     |
| RESPONSE, FORMS THE QUADRATIC REGRESSION MODEL AND ESTIMATES  |
| THE PARAMETERS, THEN SOLVES FOR THE OPTIMAL RESPONSE, PRINTS  |
| THE OPTIMAL FACTORS AND RESPONSE, AND THEN DISPLAYS THE       |
| EIGENVALUES AND EIGENVECTORS OF THE MATRIX OF QUADRATIC       |
| PARAMETER ESTIMATES TO DETERMINE IF THE SOLUTION IS A MAXIMUM |
| OR MINIMUM, OR SADDLEPOINT, AND WHICH DIRECTION HAS THE       |
| STEEPEST AND GENTLEST SLOPES.                                 |
*--------------------------------------------------------------*
| GIVEN THAT D CONTAINS THE FACTOR VARIABLES,                   |
|          AND Y CONTAINS THE RESPONSE.                         |
*--------------------------------------------------------------*/
START RSM;
  N=NROW(D);  K=NCOL(D);                /* DIMENSIONS */
  X=J(N,1,1)||D;                        /* SET UP DESIGN MATRIX */
  DO I=1 TO K;
    DO J=1 TO I;
      X=X||D[,I]#D[,J];
      END;
    END;

  BETA=SOLVE(X`*X,X`*Y);                /* SOLVE PARAMETER ESTIMATES */
  PRINT "Parameter Estimates" , BETA;

  C=BETA[1];                            /* INTERCEPT ESTIMATE */
  B=BETA[2:(K+1)];                      /* LINEAR ESTIAMTES */
  A=J(K,K,0);
  L=K+1;                                /* FORM QUADRATICS INTO MATRIX */
  DO I=1 TO K;
    DO J=1 TO I;
      L=L+1;
      A[I,J]=BETA[L,];
      END;
    END;
  A=(A+A`)*.5;                          /* SYMMETRIZE */

  XX=-.5*SOLVE(A,B);                    /* SOLVE FOR CRITICAL VALUE */
  PRINT , "Critical Factor Values" , XX;
  YOPT=C + B`*XX + XX`*A*XX;            /* COMPUTE RESPONSE AT CRITICAL VALUE */
  PRINT , "Response at Critical Value" YOPT;
```

```
CALL EIGEN(EVAL,EVEC,A);
PRINT , "Eigenvalues and Eigenvectors", EVAL, EVEC;

IF MIN(EVAL)>0 THEN PRINT , "Solution Was a Minimum";
IF MAX(EVAL)<0 THEN PRINT , "Solution Was a Maximum";
FINISH;
```

The module was run with the following sample data:

```
/* Sample Problem with Two Factors */
D={-1 -1,   -1  0,   -1  1,
    0 -1,    0  0,    0  1,
    1 -1,    1  0,    1  1};
Y={ 71.7, 75.2, 76.3, 79.2, 81.5, 80.2, 80.1, 79.1, 75.8};

RUN RSM;
```

The results are printed below:

```
                    Parameter Estimates

                          BETA
                       81.222222
                       1.9666667
                       .21666667
                       -3.933333
                         -2.225
                       -1.383333


                  Critical Factor Values

                           XX
                       .29493761
                       -.1588806

                                             YOPT
              Response at Critical Value 81.495032

                  Eigenvalues and Eigenvectors

                          EVAL
                        -.96621
                       -4.350457

                          EVEC
                -.3510761 .93634694
                .93634694 .35107607

                  Solution Was a Maximum
```

PART IV: LANGUAGE REFERENCE

SAS/IML™ Operations in Groups

SAS/IML™ Language Reference

Chapter 15
SAS/IML™ Operations in Groups

This chapter presents tables of IML operators, functions, and calls grouped according to the type of operation performed. For an alphabetical list, see Appendix 3.

Table 15.1 Arithmetic Operators

Operator	Description
–	sign reverse
+	addition
–	subtraction
#	element multiplication
##	element power
/	division
<>	element maximum
><	element minimum

Table 15.2 Comparison Operators

Operator	Description
<	less than
<=	less than or equal to
=	equal to
^=	not equal to
>	greater than
>=	greater than or equal to

Table 15.3 Logical Operators

Operator	Description
&	logical and
|	logical or
^	logical not

Table 15.4 Matrix Inquiry Functions

Function	Description
ALL	checks for all elements nonzero.
ANY	checks for any nonzero element.
LOC	finds nonzero elements of a vector.
NCOL	finds the number of columns.
NLENG	gets the length of a character element.
NROW	finds the number of rows.

Table 15.5 Scalar Functions

Function	Description
ABS	returns the absolute value.
ARCOS	returns the arc-cosine.
ARSIN	returns the arc-sine.
ATAN	returns the arc-tangent.
COS	returns the cosine.
EXP	returns the exponential.
INT	truncates to integer value.
LOG	computes the natural logarithm.
MOD	returns the modulo (remainder).
NORMAL	returns the normal random number.
PROBCHI	returns the chi-square distribution.
PROBF	returns the F distribution.
PROBIT	returns the inverse normal distribution.
PROBNORM	returns the normal distribution.
PROBT	returns the t distribution.
SIN	returns the sine.
SQRT	returns the square root.
TAN	returns the tangent.
UNIFORM	returns the uniform random number.

Table 15.6 Reduction Functions

Function	Description
MAX	returns the maximum value of a matrix.
MIN	returns the minimum value of a matrix.
SSQ	returns the sum of squares of all elements.
SUM	returns the sum of all elements.

Table 15.7   Matrix Arithmetic Operators and Functions

Operator	Description
*	matrix multiplication
@	direct product
**	matrix power
CUSUM	cumulative sum
HDIR	horizontal direct product
TRACE	sum of diagonal elements

Table 15.8   Manipulation and Reshaping Operators and Functions

Operator	Description
`	produces the transpose.
[ ]	produces subscripts.
||	performs horizontal concatenation.
//	performs vertical concatenation.
BLOCK	creates a block-diagonal matrix.
DIAG	creates a square matrix from diagonal elements.
I	creates an identity matrix.
INSERT	inserts rows or columns.
J	produces a matrix of identical values.
REMOVE	removes elements.
REPEAT	creates a matrix of repeated argument values.
SHAPE	shapes a matrix.
SQRSYM	converts symmetric to square.
SYMSQR	converts square to symmetric.
VECDIAG	creates a column vector from diagonal elements.

Table 15.9   Sequence Operator and Function

Operator	Description
:	creates an index vector.
DO	produces an arithmetic series.

Table 15.10   Ordering Functions

Function	Description
RANK	performs ranking.
RANKTIE	performs ranking with ties averaged.

Table 15.11   Character Manipulation Functions

Function	Description
BYTE	gets ASCII byte by number.
CHANGE	changes substrings.
CHAR	converts numeric to character.
CONCAT	performs elementwise concatenation.
CSHAPE	reshapes by characters.
LENGTH	finds lengths of elements.
NAME	returns the name of arguments.
NUM	converts character to numeric.
ROWCATB	concatenates elements across a row.
ROWCATC	concatenates elements across a row.
SUBSTR	produces a substring.

Table 15.12   Set Functions

Function	Description
SETDIF	finds set difference.
UNION	finds set union.
UNIQUE	removes duplicates.
XSECT	finds set intersection.

Table 15.13   Interface Functions and Calls

Function	Description
SOUND	produces sound.
VALSET	sets value by expressed name.
VALUE	gets value by expressed name.

Table 15.14   Linear Algebraic Functions and Calls

Function	Description
DET	computes the determinant.
EIGEN	computes eigenvalues and eigenvectors.
EIGVAL	computes eigenvalues.
GINV	creates the generalized inverse.
HALF	performs Cholesky decomposition.
INV	produces the inverse.
ORPOL	generates orthogonal polynomials.
ROOT	performs the Cholesky decomposition.
SOLVE	solves a system of linear equations.
SVD	performs singular value decomposition.
SWEEP	performs sweep function.

Table 15.15   Statistical Functions

Function	Description
DESIGN	creates design matrices.
DESIGNF	creates full-rank design matrices.

Table 15.16   Data Management Commands and Functions

Function	Description
APPEND	adds records at the end of the data set.
CLOSE	closes a SAS data set or external file.
CONTENTS	shows variables in a member.
CREATE	opens a new SAS data set.
DATASETS	shows members in a data library.
DELETE	deletes (erases) a SAS data set.
DELETE	marks records as deleted.
EDIT	opens a SAS data set for read and write access.
FIND	finds records satisfying conditions.
FORCE	forces out data to a data set.
LIST	displays records.
PURGE	purges deleted records from SAS data set.
READ	reads data.
RENAME	renames a SAS data set.
REPLACE	replaces data in a data set.
SETIN	selects an open data set for input.
SETOUT	selects an open data set for output.
SHOW CONTENTS	shows contents of current data set.
SHOW DATASETS	shows data sets currently active.
USE	opens a SAS data set for read access.

## Chapter 16

SAS/IML™ Language Reference

INTRODUCTION
OPERATORS
STATEMENTS AND FUNCTIONS

INTRODUCTION

This chapter presents lists of all operators, statements, and functions used in IML software for personal computers. All necessary details, such as arguments and operands, are described for each entry.

OPERATORS

Addition Operator: +

matrix1 + *matrix2*
matrix + *scalar*

The plus (+) infix operator produces a new matrix whose elements are the sums of the corresponding elements of *matrix1* and *matrix2*. For example, the element in the first row, first column of the first matrix is added to the element in the first row, first column of the second matrix. The sum becomes the element in the first row, first column of the new matrix.

In addition to adding conformable matrices, you can also use the + operator to add a matrix and a scalar. When you use the *matrix* + *scalar* (or *scalar* + *matrix*) form, the scalar value is added to each element of the matrix, producing a new matrix.

For example, let

```
A={1 2,
   3 4};
B={1 1,
   1 1};
C=A+B;
```

Then the result matrix **C** contains the values:

$$\begin{bmatrix} 2 & 3 \\ 4 & 5 \end{bmatrix} .$$

The same values result from

```
C=A+1;
```

When a missing value occurs in an operand, IML assigns a missing value for the corresponding element in the result.

Sign Reverse Operator: −

−matrix

The minus (−) prefix operator produces a new matrix whose elements are formed by reversing the sign of each element in *matrix*. For example, let

```
A={-1  7  6,
    2  0 -8};
B=-A;
```

then the result in **B** is

$$\begin{bmatrix} 1 & -7 & -6 \\ -2 & 0 & 8 \end{bmatrix} .$$

Subtraction Operator: −

matrix1 − matrix2
matrix1 − scalar

The minus (−) infix operator produces a new matrix whose elements are formed by subtracting the corresponding elements of *matrix2* from those of *matrix1*.

In addition to subtracting conformable matrices, you can also use the − operator to subtract a matrix and a scalar. When either argument is a scalar, the operation is performed by using the scalar against each element of the matrix argument.

When a missing value occurs in an operand, IML assigns a missing value for the corresponding element in the result.

Index Creation Operator: :

value1 : value2

The colon (:) operator creates a row vector whose first element is *value1*. The second element is *value1* + 1, and so on while the elements are less than or equal to *value2*. For example, the statement

```
I=7:10;
```

results in

$$\begin{array}{cccc} & & I & \\ 7 & 8 & 9 & 10 \end{array}$$

If *value1*>*value2*, an empty matrix results; in other words, I will have 0 rows and 0 columns. (Note: this is different from PROC MATRIX.)

Use the DO function if you want an increment other than 1.

Matrix Multiplication Operator: *

*matrix1 * matrix2*

The asterisk (*) infix operator produces a new matrix by performing matrix multiplication. The first matrix must have the same number of columns as the second matrix has rows. The new matrix has the same number of rows as the first matrix and the same number of columns as the second matrix.

If either matrix is a scalar, the operator performs scalar multiplication.

For example, the statements

```
A={1 2,
   3 4};
B={1 2};
C=B*A;
```

result in

$$\begin{array}{cc} & C \\ 7 & 10 \end{array}$$

and

```
D=A*B`;
```

results in

$$\begin{array}{c} D \\ 5 \\ 11 \end{array}$$

and

```
E=A*5;
```

results in

$$\begin{array}{cc} & E \\ 5 & 10 \\ 15 & 20 \end{array}$$

Element Multiplication Operator:

matrix1 # matrix2
matrix # scalar
matrix # vector

The pound sign (#) operator produces a new matrix whose elements are the products of the corresponding elements of *matrix1* and *matrix2*.

For example,

```
A={1 2,
   3 4};
B={4 8,
   0 5};
C=A#B;
```

result in

```
        C
     4        16
     0        20
```

In addition to multiplying conformable matrices, you can use the # operator to multiply a matrix and a scalar. When either argument is a scalar, the scalar value is multiplied by each element in *matrix1* to form the new matrix.

You can also multiply vectors by matrices. You can multiply matrices as long as they either conform in each dimension or one operand has dimension value 1. For example, a 2 x 3 matrix can be multiplied on either side by a 2 x 3, a 1 x 3, a 2 x 1, or a 1 x 1 matrix. Multiplying the 2 x 2 matrix **A** by the vector **D**, as in

```
D={10,100};
AD=A#D;
```

produces

```
        AD
    10        20
   300       400
```

Element multiplication with the # operator should not be confused with matrix multiplication (*). The result produced by the # operator is also known as the Schur or Hadamard product.

When a missing value occurs in an operand, IML assigns a missing value in the result.

Direct Product Operator: @

matrix1 @ matrix2

The at sign (@) operator produces a new matrix that is the Kronecker product (also called the *direct product*) of *matrix1* and *matrix2*, usually denoted by A⊗B. The number of rows in the new matrix equals the product of the number of rows in *matrix1* and the number of rows in *matrix2*; the number of columns in the new matrix equals the product of the number of columns in *matrix1* and the number of columns in *matrix2*.

For example, the statements

```
A={1 2,
   3 4};
B={0 2};
C=A@B;
```

result in

```
        C
0       2       0       4
0       6       0       8
```

and

```
D=B@A;
```

results in

```
        D
0       0       2       4
0       0       6       8
```

Division Operator: /

matrix1 / matrix2
matrix / scalar

The forward slash (/) operator divides each element of *matrix1* by the corresponding element of *matrix2* producing a matrix of quotients.

In addition to dividing elements in conformable matrices, you can also use the / operator to divide a matrix by a scalar. If either operand is a scalar, the operation does the division for each element and the scalar value.

When a missing value occurs in an operand, IML assigns a missing value for the corresponding element in the result.

If a divisor is zero, a warning is printed and the result is set to missing.

Matrix Power Operator: **

*matrix ** scalar*

The power (**) operator creates a new matrix that is *matrix* multiplied by itself *scalar* times. *Matrix* must be square; *scalar* must be an integer, greater than or equal to −1. Large scalar values cause numerical problems. If the scalar is not an integer, it is truncated to an integer. For example, the statements

```
A={1 2,
   1 1};
C=A**2;
```

result in

$$
\begin{array}{cc}
\text{C} & \\
3 & 4 \\
2 & 3
\end{array}
$$

If the matrix is symmetric, it is preferable to power its eigenvalues rather than using ** on the matrix directly (see the **EIGEN Call** later in this chapter). Note that the expression

A**(−1)

is permitted and is equivalent to INV(A).

Element Power Operator:

matrix1 ## matrix2
matrix ## scalar

The element power (##) operator creates a new matrix whose elements are the elements of *matrix1* raised to the power from the corresponding element of *matrix2*. If any value in *matrix1* is negative, the corresponding element in *matrix2* must be an integer.

In addition to handling conformable matrices, the ## operator allows either operand to be a scalar. In this case, the operation takes the power for each element and the scalar value.

For example,

A=(1 2 3);
B=A##3;

result in

$$
\begin{array}{ccc}
\text{B} & & \\
1 & 8 & 27
\end{array}
$$

The statement

B=A##.5;

results in

$$
\begin{array}{c}
\text{B} \\
1 \ 1.4142136 \ 1.7320508
\end{array}
$$

The statement

B=2##A;

results in

B

| 2 | 4 | 8 |

Comparison Operators: < > = <= >= ^=

matrix1 < matrix2
matrix1 > matrix2
matrix1 = matrix2
matrix1 <= matrix2
matrix1 >= matrix2
matrix1 ^= matrix2

Scalar values can be used instead of matrices in any of the forms shown above.

The comparison operators compare two matrices, element-by-element, and produce a new matrix that contains only zeros and ones. If an element comparison is true, the corresponding element of the new matrix is 1. If the comparison is not true, the corresponding element is 0.

For example, let

```
A={1 7 3,
   6 2 4};
```

and

```
B={0 8 2,
   4 1 3};
```

Evaluation of the expression

```
A>B
```

results in the matrix of values

$$\begin{bmatrix} 1 & 0 & 1 \\ 1 & 1 & 1 \end{bmatrix}.$$

The expression

```
A>=2
```

yields the result

$$\begin{bmatrix} 0 & 1 & 1 \\ 1 & 1 & 1 \end{bmatrix}.$$

In addition to comparing conformable matrices, you can apply the comparison operators to a matrix and a scalar. If either argument is a scalar, the comparison is between each element of the matrix and the scalar.

If the element lengths of two character operands are different, the shorter elements are padded on the right with blanks for the comparison.

If a numeric missing value occurs in an operand, IML treats it as lower than any valid number for the comparison.

The following statements illustrate the use of comparison operators:

```
IF X>=Y THEN GO TO LOOP1;
IF A=5 THEN DO;
```

Element Maximum Operator: <>

matrix1 <>´ *matrix2*

The element maximum (<>) operator compares each element of *matrix1* to the corresponding element of *matrix2*. The larger of the two values becomes the corresponding element of the new matrix that is produced.

When either argument is a scalar, the comparison is between each matrix element and the scalar.

The element maximum operator can take as operands two character matrices of the same dimensions or a character matrix and a character string. If the element lengths of the operands are different, the shorter elements are padded on the right with blanks. The element length of the result is the longer of the two operand element lengths.

When a missing value occurs in an operand, IML treats it as lower than any valid number.

Element Minimum Operator: ><

matrix1 >< *matrix2*

The element minimum (><) operator compares each element of *matrix1* with the corresponding element of *matrix2*. The smaller of the values becomes the corresponding element of the new matrix that is produced.

When either argument is a scalar, the comparison is between the scalar and each element of the matrix.

The element minimum operator can take as operands two character matrices of the same dimensions or a character matrix and a character string. If the element lengths of the operands are different, the shorter elements are padded on the right with blanks. The element length of the result is the longer of the two operand element lengths.

When a missing value occurs in an operand, IML treats it as lower than any valid numeric value.

Horizontal Concatenation Operator: ||

matrix1 || *matrix2*

The horizontal concatenation (||) operator produces a new matrix by horizontally joining *matrix1* and *matrix2*. *Matrix1* and *matrix2* must have the same number of rows, which is also the number of rows in the new matrix. The number of columns in the new matrix is the number of columns in *matrix1* plus the number of columns in *matrix2*.

For example,

```
A={1 1 1,
   7 7 7};
B={0 0 0,
   8 8 8};
C=A||B;
```

result in

```
C
1        1        1        0        0        0
7        7        7        8        8        8
```

Also, if

```
B={A B C,
   D E F};
```

and

```
C={"GH" "IJ",
   "KL" "MN"};
```

then

```
A=B||C;
```

results in

```
A
A  B  C  GH IJ
D  E  F  KL MN
```

You can use the horizontal concatenation operator when one of the arguments has no value. For example, if **A** has not been defined and **B** is a matrix, **A**||**B** results in a new matrix equal to **B**.

Quotation marks (") are needed only if you want to embed blanks or maintain uppercase and lowercase distinctions.

Vertical Concatenation Operator: //

matrix1 // *matrix2*

The vertical concatenation (//) operator produces a new matrix by vertically joining *matrix1* and *matrix2*. *Matrix1* and *matrix2* must have the same number of columns, which is also the number of columns in the new matrix. For example, if **A** has three rows and two columns and if **B** has four rows and two columns, then **A**//**B** produces a matrix with seven rows and two columns. Rows one, two, and three of the new matrix correspond to **A**; rows four through seven correspond to **B**.

These statements

```
A={1 1 1,
   7 7 7};
B={0 0 0,
   8 8 8};
C=A//B;
```

result in

```
C
1        1        1
7        7        7
0        0        0
8        8        8
```

Also, if

```
B={"AB" "CD",
   "EF" "GH"};
```

and

```
C={"I" "J",
   "K" "L",
   "M" "N"};
```

then

```
A=B//C;
```

produces the new matrix

```
A
AB CD
EF GH
I  J
K  L
M  N
```

You can use the vertical concatenation operator when one of the arguments has not been assigned a value. For example, if **A** has not been defined and **B** is a matrix, **A//B** results in a new matrix equal to **B**.

Logical Operators: & | ^

matrix1 **&** *matrix2*
matrix **&** *scalar*
matrix1 **|** *matrix2*
matrix **|** *scalar*
^*matrix*

The ampersand (&) logical operator compares two matrices, element-by-element, to produce a new matrix. An element of the new matrix is 1 if the corresponding elements of *matrix1* and *matrix2* are both nonzero; otherwise, it is a zero.

An element of the new matrix produced by the vertical bar (|) operator is 1 if either of the corresponding elements of *matrix1* and *matrix2* is nonzero. If both are zero, the element is zero.

The not (^) prefix operator examines each element of a matrix and produces a new matrix whose elements are ones and zeros. If an element of *matrix* equals zero, the corresponding element in the new matrix is 1. If an element of *matrix* is nonzero, the corresponding element in the new matrix is 0.

The statements below illustrate the use of these logical operators:

```
Z=X&R;
IF A | B THEN PRINT C;
IF ^M THEN LINK X1;
```

Note: the ¬ symbol is the same as the ^ symbol for ASCII and the "not" symbol for EBCDIC keyboards.

Transpose Operator: ` (backquote character)

matrix `

The transpose (`) operator (denoted by the diacritical accent mark slanting downward from left to right) exchanges the rows and columns of *matrix*, producing the transpose of *matrix*. For example, if an element in *matrix* is in the first row and second column, it is in the second row and first column of the transpose; an element in the first row and third column of *matrix* is in the third row and first column of the transpose. If *matrix* contains three rows and two columns, its transpose has two rows and three columns.

For example, if **A** is

$$\begin{bmatrix} 1 & 2 \\ 3 & 4 \\ 5 & 6 \end{bmatrix}$$

then **B=A** ` becomes

$$\begin{bmatrix} 1 & 3 & 5 \\ 2 & 4 & 6 \end{bmatrix}.$$

Subscripts: [ ]

matrix [*rows, columns*]
matrix [*elements*]

Subscripts are applied to matrices in order to select submatrices.

Rows and *columns* are expressions that evaluate to scalars or numeric vectors that contain valid subscript values of rows and columns in the argument matrix. A subscripted matrix can appear on the left side of the equal sign. The dimensions of the target submatrix must conform to the dimensions of the source matrix.

See the chapter "SAS/IML Expressions" for further information.

STATEMENTS AND FUNCTIONS

This section presents a list of all statements and functions used in IML for personal computers. All necessary details such as arguments and options are described for each entry. The general syntax of each statement or function is also given. In the syntax, optional clauses of a statement are enclosed in < > symbols. Entries are in alphabetical order.

ABORT Statement: stop execution and exit SAS/IML

ABORT;

The ABORT statement, like the STOP statement, instructs IML to stop executing statements. It also stops IML from parsing any further statements, causing IML to close its files and exit.

ABS Function: absolute value

ABS(*matrix*)

This is a scalar function that returns the absolute value of every element of the argument matrix.

ALL Function: check for all elements nonzero

ALL(*matrix*)

The ALL function returns a value of 1 if all elements in *matrix* are nonzero. If any element of *matrix* is zero, ALL returns a value of 0. Missing values are treated as zeros.

You can use ALL to express the results of a comparison operator as a single one or zero. For example, the comparison operation **A>B** yields a matrix whose elements can be either ones or zeros. All the elements of the new matrix are ones only if each element of **A** is greater than the corresponding element of **B**.

In the statement

```
IF ALL(A>B) THEN GOTO LOOP;
```

IML executes the GOTO statement only if each element of **A** is greater than the corresponding element of **B**.

ANY Function: check for any nonzero element

ANY(*matrix*)

ANY returns a value of 1 if any of the elements in *matrix* are nonzero. If all the elements of *matrix* are zeros, ANY returns a value of 0. Missing values are treated as zeros.

For the statement

```
IF ANY(A=B) THEN PRINT A B;
```

the matrices **A** and **B** are printed if some value in **A** is the same as the corresponding value in **B**.

APPEND Statement: add observation to the end of a SAS data set

APPEND <VAR *operand*> <FROM *name* <[ROWNAME=*name*]>>;

Use the APPEND statement to add data at the end of a SAS data set. The appended variables are either the variables of the VAR *operand* or variables created from the columns of the FROM matrix. The FROM clause and the VAR *operand* should not be specified together.

You can specify a ROWNAME matrix in the FROM clause to provide more descriptive row names than the default names ROW1, ROW2,..., ROW*n*. The ROWNAME option specifies the name of a character matrix. The first *nrow* values of this matrix become values of a variable with the same name in the output data set; *nrow* is the number of rows in the FROM matrix. The procedure uses the first *nrow* elements in row-major order.

If the VAR *operand* of APPEND includes matrices with more than one row and column, APPEND adds one observation for each element in the matrix with the greatest number of elements. Elements are appended in row-major order. Variables in the VAR *operand* with fewer than the maximum number of elements contribute missing values to observations after all of their elements have been used.

The default variables for APPEND when none are specified on the VAR operand are all matrices that match with respect to name and type variables in the current data set.

ARCOS Function: trigonometric arc cosine

ARCOS(*matrix*)

ARCOS is the scalar function returning the arc cosine of each element of the argument matrix. Results are in radians.

ARSIN Function: trigonometric arc sine

ARSIN(*matrix*)

ARSIN is the scalar function returning the arc sine of each element of the argument matrix. Results are in radians.

ATAN Function: trigonometric arc tangent

ATAN(*matrix*)

ATAN is the scalar function returning the arc tangent of each element of the argument matrix. Results are in radians.

BLOCK Function: form blocked-diagonal matrices

BLOCK(*matrix1,matrix2,...matrixn*)

The BLOCK function creates a new block-diagonal matrix from all the matrices specified in the argument matrices. Up to 15 matrices can be listed. The matrices are combined diagonally to form a new matrix. For example,

```
BLOCK(A,B);
```

produces a matrix of the form

$$\begin{bmatrix} A & 0 \\ 0 & B \end{bmatrix}$$

and

```
BLOCK(A,B,C);
```

produces a matrix of the form

$$\begin{bmatrix} A & 0 & 0 \\ 0 & B & 0 \\ 0 & 0 & C \end{bmatrix}.$$

The statements

```
A={2 2,
   4 4};
B={6 6,
   8 8};
C=BLOCK(A,B);
```

result in

```
C
2        2        0        0
4        4        0        0
0        0        6        6
0        0        8        8
```

BYTE Function: translate numbers to ordinal characters

BYTE(*matrix*)

The BYTE function returns a character matrix with the same shape as the numeric argument. Each element of the result is a single character whose ordinal position in the computer's character set is specified by the corresponding numeric element in the argument. These numeric elements should generally be in the range 0 to 255.

For example, in the ASCII character set,

```
A=BYTE(47);
```

sets

```
A = "/";  (the slash character)
```

while the lowercase alphabet can be generated with

```
Y=BYTE(97:122);
```

which produces

```
Y = a b c d e f g h i j k l m n o p q r s t u v w x y z
```

This function simplifies the use of special characters and control sequences that cannot be entered directly into IML source. Consult the character set tables for the computer you are using to determine the printable and control characters that are available and their ordinal positions.

CHANGE Call: change text in an array

CALL CHANGE(*matrix,old,new*);

CHANGE changes the first occurrence of the substring *old* in each element of the character array *matrix* to the form *new*. If there is no such occurrence, the element is not changed. For example,

```
A="It was a dark and stormy night.";
CALL CHANGE(A, "night","day");
```

produces

```
A="It was a dark and stormy day."
```

In the *old* operand, the following characters are reserved for a future enhancement:

% $ [ ] { } < > – ? * # @ ' ` (backquote) ^~

CHAR Function: character representation of a numeric matrix

CHAR(*matrix<,w,d>*)
CHAR(*matrix<,w>*)
CHAR(*matrix*)

CHAR takes a numeric matrix as an argument and, optionally, a field width (*w*) and a number of decimal positions (*d*). CHAR produces a character matrix whose dimensions are the same as the dimensions of the argument matrix and whose elements are character representations of the corresponding numeric elements. CHAR can take one, two, or three arguments. The first argument is the name of a numeric matrix and must always be supplied. The second argument is the field width of the result. If the second argument is not supplied, the system default field width is used. The third argument is the number of decimal positions in the result. If no third argument is supplied, the BEST representation is used.

CLOSE Statement: close a SAS data set

CLOSE *SASdataset(s)*;

This statement is used to close one or more SAS data set(s) opened with the USE, EDIT, or CREATE statements. See the chapter "SAS/IML Data Processing" for further information.

CLOSEFILE Statement: close an input or output file

> CLOSEFILE *operands*;

This statement is used to close files opened by INFILE or FILE statements. The operand should be the same as when the file was opened with an INFILE or FILE statement. Operands are either a name (for defined filenames), literals, or an expression in parentheses (for filepath). To find out what files are open, use the statement SHOW FILES;. For further information, consult the chapter "SAS/IML File Access."

CONCAT Function: elementwise string concatenation

> CONCAT(*matrix1,matrix2*)
> CONCAT(*matrix,scalar*)

CONCAT produces a character matrix whose elements are the concatenations of corresponding element strings from the character matrices *matrix1* and *matrix2*. If both arguments are nonscalar, they must conform. Otherwise, a scalar argument will be used repeatedly to concatenate to all elements of the other argument. The element length of the result equals the sum of the element lengths of the arguments. Trailing blanks of *matrix1* elements appear before *matrix2* elements in the result matrix. For example, if you specify

```
B={"AB"    "C ",
   "DE"    "FG"};
```

and

```
C={"H "    "IJ",
   " K"    "LM"};
```

then the statement

```
A=CONCAT(B,C);
```

produces the new matrix

```
         A
ABH   C IJ
DE K  FGLM
```

Quotation marks (") are needed only if you want to embed blanks or maintain uppercase and lowercase distinctions.

CONTENTS Function: obtain a list of the variables in a SAS data set

> CONTENTS( )
> CONTENTS(*memname*)
> CONTENTS(*libname,memname*)

The CONTENTS function returns a character matrix containing the variable names for the SAS data set specified by *libname* and *memname*. The argument *libname* is a character scalar containing the name of the library, and *memname* is a character scalar containing the name of the member of the library. The result is a character matrix with *n* rows, one column, and 8 characters per element, where *n* is the number of variables in the data set. The variable list is returned in alphabetical order. If only one argument is provided, IML uses it as the *memname*, and uses the default library (DEFLIB= option). If no arguments are specified, the current open input data set is used.

COS Function: trigonometric cosine

COS(*matrix*)

COS is the scalar function returning the trigonometric cosine of each element of the argument. The result is in radians.

CREATE Statement: setup a new SAS data set

CREATE *SASdataset* <VAR *operand*>;
CREATE *SASdataset* FROM *name* <[COLNAME=*name* ROWNAME=*name*]>;

This statement creates a new SAS data set. If the SAS data set is already open, this statement makes it the current output data set.

The variables in the new SAS data set are either the variables listed in the VAR *operand* or variables created from the columns of the FROM matrix. The FROM clause and the VAR *operand* should not be specified together.

See the chapter "SAS/IML Data Processing" for more details.

You can specify a COLNAME and a ROWNAME matrix in the FROM clause. The COLNAME matrix gives names other than the default names (COL1, COL2,...COL*n*) to variables in the created data set. The COLNAME option specifies the name of a character matrix. The first *ncol* values from this matrix provide the variable names in the created data set where *ncol* is the number of columns in the FROM matrix. The procedure uses the first *ncol* elements of the COLNAME matrix in row-major order.

The ROWNAME operand adds a variable to the data set to contain row titles. The operand must be a character matrix that exists and has values. The length of the data set variable is the length of a matrix element. The same ROWNAME matrix should be used on subsequent APPEND statements for this data set.

The variable types and lengths are the current attributes of the name in the VAR *operand* or of *name* in the FROM clause if the name is defined, with the default being numeric if the name is undefined and unvalued. The default, when no variables are specified, is all active variables.

For example,

```
NAME="123456789012";
SEX="M";
CREATE SAVE.CLASS VAR {NAME SEX AGE HEIGHT WEIGHT};
```

CSHAPE Function: reshape and repeat character values

CSHAPE(*matrix,nrow,ncol,size*)
CSHAPE(*matrix,nrow,ncol,size,padchar*)

The CSHAPE function shapes character matrices. It is similar to the SHAPE function except that it reshapes at the character level. The dimensions of the matrix created by CSHAPE are specified by *nrow* (number of rows), *ncol* (number of columns), and *size* (element length). A padding character is specified by *padchar*.

CSHAPE works by looking at the source matrix as if the characters of the source elements had been concatenated in row-major order. The source characters are then regrouped into elements of length *size*. These elements are then assigned to the result matrix, once again in row-major order. If there are not enough characters for the result matrix, the source of the remaining characters depends on whether or not padding was specified with *padchar*. If no padding was specified, the source matrix's characters are cycled through again. Otherwise, the remaining characters are all the padding character. Note the following examples:

```
R=CSHAPE('abcd',2,2,1);
```

results in

$$\mathbf{R} = \begin{bmatrix} a & b \\ c & d \end{bmatrix}.$$

```
R=CSHAPE('a',1,2,3);
```

results in

$$\mathbf{R} = \begin{bmatrix} aaa & aaa \end{bmatrix}.$$

```
R=CSHAPE({'ab' 'cd',
          'ef' 'gh',
          'ij' 'kl'}, 2, 2, 3);
```

results in

$$\mathbf{R} = \begin{bmatrix} abc & def \\ ghi & jkl \end{bmatrix}.$$ (reshaping)

```
R=CSHAPE('XO' ,3,1,3);
```

results in

$$\mathbf{R} = \begin{bmatrix} X & O & X \\ O & X & O \\ X & O & X \end{bmatrix}.$$ (cycling)

```
R=CSHAPE({'ab' 'cd' ,
          'ef' 'gh',
          'ij' 'kl'},2, 1, 5);
```

results in

$$R = \begin{bmatrix} abcde \\ fghij \end{bmatrix} .$$ (truncation)

```
R=CSHAPE('abcd',2,2,3,'*');
```

results in

$$R = \begin{bmatrix} abc & d** \\ *** & *** \end{bmatrix} .$$ (padding)

CUSUM Function: cumulative sum

CUSUM(*matrix*)

The CUSUM function returns a matrix the same shape as the argument that contains the cumulative sums obtained by scanning the argument, summing in row-major order.

For example,

```
A=CUSUM(( 1 2 4 5));
B=CUSUM(( 5 6, 3 4));
```

sets

$$A = \begin{bmatrix} 1 & 3 & 7 & 12 \end{bmatrix}$$

$$B = \begin{bmatrix} 5 & 11 \\ 14 & 18 \end{bmatrix} .$$

DATASETS Function: obtain names of the SAS data sets in a SAS data library

DATASETS(*libname*)
DATASETS( )

The DATASETS function returns a character matrix containing the names of the SAS data sets in the specified library. *libname* is a character scalar containing the name of the library. The result is a character matrix with *n* rows and one column, where *n* is the number of data sets in the library. If no argument is specified, IML uses the default libname (See the DEFLIB= option in the **RESET Statement**.)

DELETE Statement: delete records

DELETE *range where*;

Use the DELETE statement to mark records for deletion in the current output data set. The *range* and *where* clauses are optional and can be specified in any order.

For example,

`DELETE;`	deletes the current observation
`DELETE POINT 34;`	deletes observation 34
`SETOUT SAVE.CLASS POINT 34;` `DELETE;`	also deletes observation 34
`DELETE ALL WHERE(AGE<21);`	deletes all observations where age<21

See the chapter "SAS/IML Data Processing" for more details.

DELETE Subroutine: delete a SAS data set

CALL DELETE(*libname,memname*);
CALL DELETE(*memname*);

The DELETE subroutine deletes a SAS data set (or data set member) in the specified library. The argument *libname* is a character scalar containing the SAS data library name; *memname* is a character scalar containing the name of the member to be deleted. If only one argument is specified, *libname* is the default libname (See the DEFLIB= option in the **RESET Statement**.)

DESIGN Function: design matrices

DESIGN(*columnvector*)

The DESIGN function creates a full-design matrix from *columnvector*. Each unique value of the vector generates a column of the design matrix. This column contains ones in elements whose corresponding elements in the vector are the current value; zeros elsewhere. The columns are arranged in the sort order of the original values.

For the column vector in the statement

```
A={1,1,2,2,3,1};
```

the resultant design matrix contains the values

$$
\begin{bmatrix}
1 & 0 & 0 \\
1 & 0 & 0 \\
0 & 1 & 0 \\
0 & 1 & 0 \\
0 & 0 & 1 \\
1 & 0 & 0
\end{bmatrix}.
$$

DESIGNF Function: full-rank design matrices

DESIGNF(*columnvector*)

The DESIGNF function works similarly to the DESIGN function; however, the result matrix is one column smaller and can be used to produce full-rank design matrices. The result of DESIGNF is the same as if you took the last column off the DESIGN function result and subtracted it from the other columns of the result.

For example, for the *columnvector* in the statement

```
A={1,1,2,2,3,3};
```

the DESIGNF function returns

```
            A
    1               0
    1               0
    0               1
    0               1
   -1              -1
   -1              -1
```

DET Function: determinant

DET(*matrix*)

The DET function computes the determinant of *matrix*, which must be square. The determinant, the product of the eigenvalues, is a single numeric value.

The method performs an LU decomposition and collects the product of the diagonals (Forsythe and Moler, 1967).

DIAG Function: diagonal

DIAG(*squarematrix*)
DIAG(*vector*)

The DIAG function creates a matrix with diagonal elements equal to the corresponding diagonal elements in *squarematrix*. All off-diagonal elements in the new matrix are zeros.

If the argument is a vector, DIAG creates a matrix whose diagonal elements are the values in the vector. All off-diagonal elements are 0.

For example, the statements

```
A={4 3,
   2 1};
B={1 2 3};
C=DIAG(A);
```

result in

```
            C
    4               0
    0               1
```

and

```
D=DIAG(B);
```

results in

```
        D
        1        0        0
        0        2        0
        0        0        3
```

DISPLAY Statement: display fields in display windows

DISPLAY <*groupspec groupoptions*>,... ;

The DISPLAY statement directs IML to gather data into fields defined on the screen for purposes of display, data entry, or menu selection. The display statement always refers to a window that has been previously opened by a WINDOW statement. The statement is described completely in the chapter "SAS/IML Display Features." Here is a summary of the syntax and features:

groupspec

is the specification of a group, either a compound name of the form *windowname.groupname* or a window name followed by a group defined by fields and enclosed in parentheses:

windowname.groupname

or

windowname (*fieldspecs*)

where *fieldspecs* is as defined for the WINDOW statement.

groupoptions

can be any of the following:

NOINPUT

requests that IML display the group with all fields protected so that no data entry can be done to the fields.

REPEAT

specifies that IML repeat the group for each element of the matrices specified as field operands.

BELL

rings the bell, sounds the alarm, or beeps the speaker on your workstation when the window is displayed.

DO Function: produce an arithmetic series

INDEX=DO(*start,stop,increment*)

The DO function creates a row vector containing a sequence of numbers starting with *start* and incrementing by *increment* as long as the elements are less than or equal to *stop* (greater than or equal to *stop* for a negative increment). This function is a generalization of the : operator.

For example,

```
I=DO(3,18,3);
```

yields the result

$$\begin{bmatrix} 3 & 6 & 9 & 12 & 15 & 18 \end{bmatrix}$$.

DO and END Statements: grouping

DO;
    statements
    END;

The DO statement specifies that the statements following the DO statement are to be executed as a group until a matching END statement appears. DO statements usually appear in IF-THEN and ELSE statements where they designate groups of statements to be performed when the IF condition is true or false.

For example, the statements

```
IF X=Y THEN DO;
   I=I+L;
   PRINT X;
   END;
PRINT Y;
```

specify that the statements between the DO and the END statements (the DO group) are to be performed only if X=Y. If X is not equal to Y, the statements in the DO group are skipped and the next statement executed is

```
PRINT Y;
```

DO groups can be nested. Any number of nested DO groups is allowed. Here is an example of nested DO statements:

```
IF Y>Z THEN DO;
   IF Z=0 THEN DO;
      Z=B+C;
      END;
   X=Z#R;
   END;
```

It is good practice to indent the statements in a DO group as shown so that their positions indicate their levels of nesting.

DO Groups: iterative execution

DO *variable*=*start* TO *stop*;
DO *variable*=*start* TO *stop* BY *increment*;

When the DO group has one of these forms, the statements between the DO and the END are executed repetitively. The number of times the statements are executed depends on the evaluation of the expressions given in the DO statement.

The *start*, *stop*, and *increment* values should be scalars or expressions whose evaluation yields scalars. The *variable* is given a new value for each repetition of the group. The index variable starts with the *start* value, then is incremented by the *increment* value each time. The iterations continue as long as the index variable is less than or equal to the *stop* value. If a negative increment is used, then the rules reverse so that the index variable decrements to a lower bound.

To study how the iterations are controlled, look at these equivalent sections of code. The first section is done with an iterative DO group; the second performs the same task using other statements such as IF and GOTO.

```
DO I=start TO stop BY increment;
   statements
   END;
Z: more statements
```

The above code is equivalent to:

```
   I=start;                    /* STARTING VALUE    */
   DOLIM=stop;                 /* REMEMBER BOUND    */
   DOINC=increment;            /* REMEMBER INCREMENT */
L:IF I>DOLIM THEN GO TO Z;     /* CHECK INDEX>BOUND? */
   statements
   I=I+DOINC;                  /* INCREMENTING */
   GO TO L;                    /* ITERATE BACK */

Z: more statements             /* CONTINUE AFTER THE LOOP*/
```

Note that the *start, stop,* and *increment* expressions are evaluated only once before the looping starts.

DO Statement with DATA Clause

```
DO DATA;
DO DATA variable=start TO stop;
```

The DATA keyword is used for repetitive DO loops that need to be exited upon the occurrence of an end-of-file for an INPUT or READ or other I/O statement. This form is common for loops that read data.

When an end of file is reached inside the DO DATA group, IML immediately jumps from the group and starts executing the statement following the END statement in the group. DO DATA groups can be nested, where each end of file causes a jump from the most local DO DATA group. The keyword DATA is mnemonic of the end-of-file behavior or the SAS Data Step.

DO Statement with UNTIL Clause

```
DO UNTIL(expression);
DO variable=start TO stop UNTIL(expression);
DO variable=start TO stop BY increment UNTIL(expression);
```

Using a WHILE expression makes possible the conditional execution of a set of statements iteratively. The UNTIL expression is evaluated at the bottom of the loop, and the statements inside the loop are executed repeatedly as long as the expression yields a zero or missing value.

DO Statement with WHILE Clause

DO WHILE(*expression*);
DO *variable*=*start* TO *stop* WHILE(*expression*);
DO *variable*=*start* TO *stop* BY *increment* WHILE(*expression*);

Using a WHILE expression makes possible the conditional execution of a set of statements iteratively. The WHILE expression is evaluated at the top of the loop, and the statements inside the loop are executed repeatedly as long as the expression yields a nonzero or nonmissing value.

The statements

```
L: DO I=start TO stop BY increment WHILE(expression);
     IML statements
     END;
Z: more statements
```

are equivalent to the statements

```
L: I=start;                          /* STARTING VALUE    */
   DOLIM=stop;                       /* REMEMBER BOUND    */
   DOINC=increment;                  /* REMEMBER INCREMENT*/
   GO TO IN;                         /* SKIP INCREMENTING FIRST TIME*/
REPEAT:I=I+DOINC;                    /* INCREMENTING      */
   IN: IF I>DOLIM THEN GO TO Z;      /* CHECK INDEX>BOUND */
       IF ^expression THEN GO TO Z;  /* CHECK WHILE EXPRESSION*/
       IML statements
       GO TO REPEAT;
   Z: more IML statements            /* CONTINUE AFTER THE LOO P */
```

Note that the incrementing is done before the WHILE expression is tested.

EDIT Statement: open a SAS data set for editing

EDIT *SASdataset* <*range*> <VAR *operand*> <WHERE(*whereexpr*)>;

This statement opens a SAS data set for reading and updating. If the data set has already been opened, the statement makes it the current input and output data sets.

You can use EDIT to define a set of variables or to define the selection criteria used to control access to data set observations.

The *range*, VAR, and WHERE clauses are optional and can be specified in any order.

See the chapter "SAS/IML Data Processing" for further details.

EIGEN Call: eigenvalues and eigenvectors

CALL EIGEN(*eigenvalues*,*eigenvectors*,*symmetricmatrix*);

The EIGEN subroutine creates *eigenvalues*, a vector containing the eigenvalues of *symmetricmatrix* arranged in descending order. EIGEN also creates *eigenvectors*,a matrix containing the orthonormal column eigenvectors of *symmetricmatrix* arranged so that the matrices are correspondent.

The results of

```
CALL EIGEN(M,E,A);
```

have the properties:

    A*E=E*diag(M)
    E'*E=I(N)

that is,

    E'=INV(E)   .

Thus,

    A=E*diag(M)*E'   .

The QL method is used to compute the eigenvalues (Wilkinson and Reinsch, 1971).

IML cannot directly compute the eigenvalues of a general nonsymmetric matrix because some of the eigenvalues may be imaginary. In statistical applications, nonsymmetric matrices for which eigenvalues are desired are usually of the form $E^{-1} H$, where E and H are symmetric. The eigenvalues L and eigenvectors V of $E^{-1} H$ can be obtained as follows:

```
F=ROOT(EINV);
A=F*H*F';
CALL EIGEN(L,W,A);
V=F'*W;
```

The computation can be checked by forming the residuals:

```
R=EINV*H*V-V*DIAG(L);
```

The values in R should be of the order of round-off error.

EIGVAL Function: eigenvalues

    EIGVAL(*symmetricmatrix*)

The EIGVAL function creates a column vector of the eigenvalues of *symmetricmatrix*. The eigenvalues are arranged in descending order. See **EIGEN Call** for more details.

END Statement

    END;

See **DO and END Statements** above.

EXP Function: exponential

    EXP(*matrix*)

This scalar function takes the exponential function of every element of the argument matrix. Exponential can be defined as taking the natural number e raised to the indicated power.

FILE Statement: open or point to external file

    FILE *fileoperand options... ;*

You can use the FILE statement to open a file for output, or if the file is already open, to make it the current output file so that subsequent PUT statements write to it. The FILE statement is similar in syntax and operation to the INFILE statement. The FILE statement is described in detail in the chapter "SAS/IML File Access."

The *fileoperand* is either a predefined filename or a quoted string or character expression in parentheses referring to the file path. See the section **File Naming** in the "SAS/IML File Access" chapter for details on specifying a file name.

The *options* available for the FILE statement are

RECFM=U

> specifies that the file is to be written as a pure binary file without record separator characters.

LRECL=*operand*

> specifies the size of the buffer to hold the records. The default size 512 is enough for most applications.

FIND Statement: find records

> FIND *range* WHERE(*whereexpression*) INTO *name*;

You can use this data processing statement to find observations in *range* that satisfy the conditions of the WHERE clause. FIND places these observation numbers in the numeric matrix whose name follows the INTO keyword. The INTO clause is required.

For example,

```
FIND ALL  WHERE(NAME=:"Smith") INTO P;
FIND NEXT WHERE(AGE>30) INTO P2;
```

See the chapter "SAS/IML Data Processing" for further details.

FINISH Statement: end of module

> FINISH;

The FINISH statement signals the end of a module and the end of module definition mode. See the **START Statement** later in this chapter, and consult the chapter "SAS/IML Programming Statements" for further information.

FORCE Statement: force out data

> FORCE;

You can use the FORCE statement to force out any data residing in output buffers for all active output data sets and files to ensure that the data are written to disk. This is equivalent to closing and then reopening the files.

FREE Statement: free matrix storage space

> FREE *matrix*;
> FREE *matrix1 matrix2...matrixn*;
> FREE /;
> FREE / *matrices*;

The FREE statement causes the specified matrices to lose their values; the memory is then freed for other uses. After execution of FREE, the matrix does not have a value, and it returns 0 for NROW and NCOL functions. Any printing attributes (assigned by MATTRIB) are not released.

The FREE statement is used mostly in large applications to make room for more values.

If you want to free all matrices, specify a slash (/) after the command FREE. If you want to free all matrices except a few specified, then list the ones you do not want to free after the slash.

GINV Function: generalized inverse

GINV(*matrix*)

The GINV function creates the Moore-Penrose generalized inverse of *matrix*. This inverse, known as the four-condition inverse, has these properties:
If

$$G = GINV(A)$$

then

$$AGA = A$$
$$GAG = G$$
$$(AG)' = AG$$
$$(GA)' = GA \quad .$$

The inverse is also known as the *pseudoinverse*, usually denoted by A^+. It is computed using the singular value decomposition (Wilkinson and Reinsch 1971).
Least-squares regression for the model

$$Y = X\beta + \varepsilon$$

can be performed by using

```
B=GINV(X)*Y;
```

This solution has minimum **B'B** among all solutions minimizing $\varepsilon`\varepsilon$.

Projection matrices can be formed by specifying GINV(**X**)*X (*row space*) or **X***GINV(**X**) (*column space*).

See Rao and Mitra (1971) for a discussion of properties of this function.

GOTO Statement

GOTO *label*;

The GOTO (or GO TO) statement directs IML to jump immediately to the statement with the given *label* and begin executing statements from that point. Any IML statement can have a label, which is a name followed by a colon preceding any executable statement.

GOTO statements are usually clauses of conditional IF statements. For example,

```
    IF X>Y THEN GOTO SKIP;
    Y=LOG(Y-X);
    YY=Y-20;
  SKIP: more statements
```

The function of GOTO statements is usually better performed by DO groups. For example, the statements above could be better written:

```
IF X<=Y THEN DO;
   Y=LOG(Y-X);
   YY=Y-20;
   END;
more statements
```

You should avoid GOTO statements when they refer to a label above the GOTO statement; otherwise, an infinite loop is possible.

HALF Function: Cholesky decomposition

The HALF function has been replaced by the ROOT function. See the **ROOT Function** later in this chapter for Cholesky decomposition.

HDIR Function: horizontal direct product

HDIR(*matrix1,matrix2*)

The HDIR function performs a direct product on all rows of *matrix1* and *matrix2* and creates a new matrix by stacking these row vectors into a matrix. This operation is useful in constructing design matrices of interaction effects. *Matrix1* and *matrix2* must have the same number of rows. The result has the same number of rows as *matrix1* and *matrix2*. The number of columns is equal to the product of the number of columns in *matrix1* and *matrix2*.

For example, the statements

```
A={1 2,
   2 4,
   3 6 };
B={0  2,
   1  1,
   0 -1 };
C=HDIR(A,B);
```

produce a matrix containing the values

$$\begin{bmatrix} 0 & 2 & 0 & 4 \\ 2 & 2 & 4 & 4 \\ 0 & -3 & 0 & -6 \end{bmatrix}.$$

HDIR is useful for constructing crossed and nested effects from main effect design matrices in ANOVA models.

I Function: identity matrix

I(*dimension*)

The I function creates an identity matrix with *dimension* rows and columns. The diagonal elements of an identity matrix are ones; all other elements are zeros. The value of *dimension* must be an integer greater than or equal to 1.

For example,

```
A=I(3);
```

yields the result

$$\begin{bmatrix} 1 & 0 & 0 \\ 0 & 1 & 0 \\ 0 & 0 & 1 \end{bmatrix}.$$

IF-THEN and ELSE Statements

IF *expression* THEN *statement*;
ELSE *statement*;

IF statements contain an expression to be evaluated, the keyword THEN, and an action to be taken when the result of the evaluation has a true value.

The ELSE statement follows the IF statement. ELSE gives an action to be taken when the IF expression is false. The expression to be evaluated is often a comparison. For example,

```
IF MAX(A)<20 THEN P=0;
ELSE P=1;
```

The IF statement results in the evaluation of the condition (MAX(A)<20). If the largest value found in matrix A is less than 20, P is set to 0. Otherwise, P is set to 1. See the MAX Function.

When the condition to be evaluated is a matrix expression, the result of the evaluation is another matrix. If all values of the result matrix are nonzero and non-missing, the condition is true; if any element in the result matrix is 0 or missing, the condition is false. This evaluation is equivalent to using the ALL function.

For example, writing

```
IF X<Y THEN DO;
```

produces the same result as writing

```
IF ALL(X<Y) THEN DO;
```

IF statements can be nested within the clauses of other IF or ELSE statements. Any number of nesting levels is allowed. For example,

```
IF X=Y THEN IF ABS(Y)=Z THEN DO;
```

Caution

The expressions

```
IF A^=B THEN...;
```

and

```
IF ^(A=B) THEN...;
```

are valid, but the THEN clause in each case is only executed when all correspond-ing elements of A and B are unequal.

Evaluation of the expression

```
IF ANY(A^=B) THEN... ;
```

requires only one element of **A** and **B** to be unequal for the expression to be true.

INDEX Statement: index a variable on a data set

INDEX *names...* ;

You can use this statement to create an index for the named variables in the cur-rent input SAS data set. An index is created for each variable listed. Subsequent operations with WHERE clauses can use these indexes to locate data. The INDEX statement can take a long time if the data set is large.

INFILE Statement: opening files for input

INFILE *infileoperand options...* ;

You can use the INFILE statement to open a data set for input or, if the file is already open, to make it the current input file so that subsequent INPUT state-ments read from it.

The *infileoperand* is either a predefined filename or a quoted string or character expression in parentheses referring to the file path. See the section **File Naming** in the chapter "SAS/IML File Access" for further information.

The *options* available for the INFILE statement are

RECFM=U

specifies that the file is to be read in as a pure binary file rather than as a file with record separator characters. To do this, you must use the < feature to get new records rather than using separate input statements or the / operator.

LENGTH=L

specifies a variable where the length of a record will be stored as IML reads it in.

LRECL=*operand*

specifies the size of the buffer to hold the records. The default size 512 is enough for most applications.

The following options control how IML behaves when an input statement tries to read past the end of a record. The default is STOPOVER.

MISSOVER

tolerates attempted reading past the end of the record by assigning missing values to variables read past the end of the record.

FLOWOVER

allows the input statement to go to the next record to obtain values for the variables.

STOPOVER

treats going past the end of a record as an error condition, which will trigger an end-of-file condition.

INPUT Statement: inputting data from files

INPUT *items...* ;

You can use the INPUT statement to input records from the current input file, placing the values into IML variables. The INFILE statement sets up the current input file. See the chapter "SAS/IML File Access" for details.

The INPUT statement contains a sequence of items that include the following:

record-directives
> are used to advance to a new record. Record-directives include:
>
> /
>> instructs IML to advance to the next record.
>
> \> *operand*
>> specifies that the next record to be read starts at the indicated byte position in the file (for RECFM=U files only). The *operand* is a literal number, a variable name, or an expression in parentheses.
>
> \< *operand*
>> instructs IML to read in the indicated number of bytes as the next record (for RECFM=U files only). The *operand* is a literal number, a variable name, or an expression in parentheses.

positionals
> instruct the system to go to a specific column on the record. These include:
>
> @ *operand*
>> instructs IML to go to the indicated column, where *operand* is a literal number, a variable name, or an expression in parentheses. For example @30 means to go to column 30. The operand can also be a character operand when pattern searching is needed.
>
> + *operand*
>> specifies that the indicated number of columns are to be skipped. The *operand* is a literal number, a variable name, or an expression in parentheses.

inputvariable
> specifies the variable you want to read into from the current position in the record. The *inputvariable* can be followed immediately by an input format specification.

informat
> specifies an input format. These are of the form *w.d* or $*w*. for standard numeric and character informats where *w* is the width of the field and *d* is the decimal parameter, if any. You can also use a named format of the form: NAME*w.d* where NAME is the name of the format. Also, you can use a single $ or & for list input applications. If the width is unspecified, the informat uses LIST-input rules to determine the length by searching for a blank (or comma) delimiter. A special format $RECORD. is used for reading in the rest of the record into one variable.

holding @ sign
> is used at the end of an input statement to instruct IML to hold the current record so that you can continue to read from the record with

later input statements. Otherwise, IML automatically goes to the next record for the next input statement.

Record holding is always implied for RECFM=U binary files, as if the INPUT statement has a trailing @ sign.

INSERT Function: matrix insertion

INSERT(*x,y,row*)
INSERT(*x,y,row,col*)

The INSERT function returns the result of inserting the matrix *y* inside the matrix *x* at the place specified by the *row* and *column* arguments. This is done by splitting *x* either horizontally or vertically before the row or column specified and concatenating *y* between the two pieces. Thus, if *x* is *m* rows x *n* columns, *row* can range from zero to *m*+1 and *col* can range from zero to *n*+1. However, it is not possible to insert in both dimensions simultaneously, so either *row* or *col* must be 0, but not both. The column argument is optional and defaults to 0. Also, the matrices must conform in the dimension in which they are joined.

For example,

```
A={1 2, 3 4};
B={5 6, 7 8};
C=INSERT(A, B, 2, 0);
D=INSERT(A, B, 0, 3);
```

produces

$$C = \begin{bmatrix} 1 & 2 \\ 5 & 6 \\ 7 & 8 \\ 3 & 4 \end{bmatrix}$$

$$D = \begin{bmatrix} 1 & 2 & 5 & 6 \\ 3 & 4 & 7 & 8 \end{bmatrix}$$

C shows the result of inserting in the middle, while **D** shows insertion on an end. On the other hand,

```
A={1 2 3, 4 5 6};
B={5 6, 7 8};
C=INSERT(A, B, 2, 0);
```

produces an error since **A** and **B** do not have the same number of columns. However,

```
D=INSERT(A, B, 0, 2);
```

works since **A** and **B** do conform in the row dimension, producing

$$D=\begin{bmatrix} 1 & 5 & 6 & 2 & 3 \\ 4 & 7 & 8 & 5 & 6 \end{bmatrix} .$$

INT Function: integer value

INT(*matrix*)

INT is a scalar function taking the integer value of each element of the argument matrix.

INV Function: matrix inverse

INV(*matrix*)

INV produces a matrix that is the inverse of *matrix*, which must be square and nonsingular.

For **G**=INV(**A**) the inverse has the properties:

GA=**AG**=identity .

To solve a system of linear equations **AX**=**B** for **X**, you can use

```
X=INV(A)*B;
```

However, the SOLVE function is more accurate and efficient for this use.

The INV function uses an LU decomposition followed by backsubstitution to solve for the inverse, as described in Forsythe and Moler (1967).

J Function: matrix of identical values

J(*nrow*)
J(*nrow,ncol*)
J(*nrow,ncol,value*)

The J function creates a matrix with *nrow* rows and *ncol* columns with all elements equal to *value*. If *ncol* is not specified, it defaults to *nrow*. If *value* is not specified, it defaults to 1. The REPEAT and SHAPE functions can also serve this operation, and they are more general.

LENGTH Function: lengths of character matrix elements

LENGTH(*matrix*)

The LENGTH function takes a character matrix as an argument and produces a numeric matrix as a result. The result matrix has the same dimensions as the argument and contains the lengths of the corresponding string elements in *matrix*. The length of a string is equal to the position of the rightmost nonblank character in the string. If a string is entirely blank, its length value is set to 1.

LINK and RETURN Statements

LINK *label*;
    statements
label: *statements*
RETURN;

The LINK statement, like the GOTO statement, directs IML to jump to the statement with the specified label. Unlike the GOTO statement, IML remembers where the LINK was issued and returns to that point when a RETURN statement is executed.

LINK provides a way of calling sections of code as if they were subroutines. The LINK statement calls the routine. The routine begins with the label and ends with a RETURN statement. LINK statements can be nested within other LINK statements to any level. A RETURN statement without a LINK is executed just like the STOP statement.

Any time you use LINK, you may consider using RUN and a START/FINISH defined module instead.

LIST Statement: display records

LIST <range> <VAR operand> <WHERE(whereexpr)>;

Use the LIST statement to display data. If all data values for variables in VAR fit on a single line, values are displayed in columns headed by the variable names. Each record occupies a separate line. If the data values do not fit on a single line, values from each record are grouped into paragraphs. Each element in the paragraph has the form name=value.

For example,

```
LIST ALL;                 lists whole data set
LIST;                     lists current observation
LIST VAR{NAME ADDR};      lists specified variables in current obs
LIST ALL WHERE(AGE>30);   lists observations where condition holds
LIST NEXT;                lists next observation
LIST POINT 24;            lists observation 24
LIST POINT (10:15);       lists observations 10 through 15
```

For more information, see the "SAS/IML Data Processing" chapter.

LOAD Statement: load from disk storage

```
LOAD;
LOAD names... ;
```

The LOAD statement loads matrix values from the disk library storage into the current workspace. If no names are given, IML loads all matrices stored in the library storage. For more information, see the "SAS/IML Library Storage" chapter.

LOC Function: find nonzero elements of a matrix

LOC(matrix)

The LOC function creates a 1 x n row vector where n is the number of nonzero elements in the argument. Missing values are treated as zeros. The values in the resulting row vector are the locations of the nonzero elements in the argument (in row-major order, like subscripting). For example, suppose

```
A={1 0 2 3 0};
```

then

```
B=LOC(A);
```

results in

```
        B
        1      3      4
```

since the first, third, and fourth elements of **A** are nonzero. If every element of
the argument vector is 0, the result is empty; that is, **B** has 0 rows and 0 columns.

The LOC function is useful for subscripting parts of a matrix that satisfy some
condition. For example, suppose you want to create a matrix **Y** that contains the
rows of **X** having a positive element in the diagonal of **X**.

Let

```
X={1   1   0,
   0  -2   2,
   0   0   3};
```

then

```
Y=X[LOC(VECDIAG(X)>0),];
```

results in

    Y=**X**[{1 3},]

or

```
        Y
        1      1      0
        0      0      3
```

since the first and third rows of **X** have positive elements on the diagonal of **X**.

To select all positive elements of a column vector

```
A={0,
  -1,
   2,
   0 };
```

the statement

```
Y=A[LOC(A>0),];
```

results in

    Y=**A**[3,]

or

```
        Y
        2
```

LOG Function: natural logarithm

LOG(*matrix*)

LOG is the scalar function that takes the natural logarithm of each element of the argument matrix.

MATTRIB Statement

MATTRIB *name* ROWNAME=*name* COLNAME=*name*;

The MATTRIB statement associates printing attributes with matrices. Each matrix can be associated with a ROWNAME matrix and a COLNAME matrix, which is used whenever the matrix is printed to label the rows and columns, respectively. The statement is written as the keyword MATTRIB followed by a list of names and attribute associations. The attribute associations are applied to the previous *name*. Thus, the statement

```
MATTRIB A ROWNAME=RA COLNAME=CA B COLNAME=CB;
```

gives a ROWNAME and a COLNAME to **A**, and a COLNAME to **B**.

You cannot group names; although the following statement is valid, it does not associate anything with **A**:

```
MATTRIB A B ROWNAME=N;
```

The values of the associated matrices are not looked up until they are needed. Thus, they need not be given values at the time the MATTRIB statement is specified. They can be specified later when the object matrix is printed. The attributes continue to bind with the matrix until reassigned with another MATTRIB statement. To eliminate an attribute, specify EMPTY as the name, for example, ROWNAME=EMPTY.

MAX Function: maximum value of matrix

MAX(*matrix*)
MAX(*matrix1,matrix2,....matrixn*)

MAX produces a single numeric value (or a character string value) that is the largest element (or highest character string value) in all arguments. There can be as many as fifteen argument matrices. The function checks for missing numeric values and does not include them in the result. If all arguments are missing, then the machine's most negative representable number is the result.

If you want to find the elementwise maximums of the corresponding elements of two matrices, use the <> operator.

The length of the character string is to be the longest element length among the argument matrices.

MIN Function: minimum value of matrix

MIN(*matrix*)
MIN(*matrix1,matrix2,...matrixn*)

MIN produces a single numeric value (or a character string value) that is the smallest element (lowest character string value) in all arguments. There can be as many as fifteen argument matrices. The function checks for missing numeric values and excludes them from the result. If all arguments are missing, then the machine's largest representable number is the result.

If you want to find the elementwise minimums of the corresponding elements of two matrices, use the $><$ operator.

The length of the character string is the longest element length among the argument matrices.

MOD Function: modulo (remainder)

MOD(*value,divisor*)

MOD is the scalar function returning the remainder of the division of elements of the first argument by elements of the second argument.

NAME Function: names of arguments

NAME(*argument,argument,...*)

NAME returns the names of the arguments in a column vector. In the example,

```
N=NAME(A,B,C);
```

N would become a 3 row by 1 column character matrix of element size 8 containing the character values A, B, and C.

NAME has one main use. You can use NAME in macros when you want to use an argument for both its name and value.

NCOL Function: number of columns

NCOL(*matrix*)

NCOL returns a single numeric value that is the number of columns in *matrix*. If the matrix has not been given a value, NCOL returns a value of 0.

NLENG Function: size of an element

NLENG(*matrix*)

NLENG returns a single numeric value that is the size in bytes of each element in *matrix*. All matrix elements have the same size. If the matrix does not have a value, then NLENG returns a value of 0.

NORMAL Function: pseudo-random normal deviate

NORMAL(*seed*)

NORMAL is the scalar function returning a pseudo-random number having a normal distribution with mean zero and standard deviation of 1. The NORMAL function returns a matrix with the same dimensions as the argument. The first argument on the first call is used for the seed—or if that is zero, the system clock is used for the seed.

NROW Function: number of rows

NROW(*matrix*)

NROW returns a single numeric value that is the number of rows in matrix. If the matrix has not been given a value, NROW returns a value of 0.

NUM Function: numeric representation of character matrix

NUM(*matrix*)

NUM takes as an argument a character matrix whose elements are character numerics and produces a numeric matrix whose dimensions are the same as the dimensions of the argument and whose elements are the numeric representations (double-precision floating point) of the corresponding elements of the argument.

OPSCAL Function: rescales qualitative data to be a least-squares fit to quantitative data

OPSCAL(MLEVEL,QUANTI)
OPSCAL(MLEVEL,QUANTI,QUALIT)

The result of the OPSCAL function is the optimal scaling transformation of the qualitative (nominal or ordinal) data in QUALIT. The optimal scaling transformation result

- is a least squares fit to the quantitative data in QUANTI.
- preserves the qualitative measurement level of QUALIT.

OPSCAL performs as a function or call. When used as a call, the first argument of the call is the matrix to contain the result returned.

You can use the following arguments with OPSCAL:

MLEVEL   specifies a scalar that can have only two values. When MLEVEL=1 the QUALIT matrix is at the nominal measurement level; when MLEVEL=2 it is at the ordinal measurement level.

QUANTI   specifies an $m \times n$ matrix of quantitative information assumed to be at the interval level of measurement.

QUALIT   specifies an $m \times n$ matrix of qualitative information whose level of measurement is specified by MLEVEL. When QUALIT is omitted, MLEVEL must be 2. When omitted, a temporary QUALIT is constructed that contains the integers from 1 to n in the first row, from $n+1$ to $2n$ in the second row, from $2n+1$ to $3n$ in the third row, and so forth, up to the integers $(m-1)n$ to mn in the last (mth) row. Note that you cannot specify QUALIT as a character matrix.

When QUALIT is at the nominal level of measurement, the optimal scaling transformation result is a least-squares fit to QUANTI, given the restriction that the category structure of QUALIT must be preserved. If element i of QUALIT is in category c, then element i of the optimum scaling transformation result is the mean of all those elements of QUANTI that correspond to elements of QUALIT that are in category c. For example, consider these statements:

```
QUANTI = { 5  4  6  7  4  6  2  4  8  6 };
QUALIT = { 6  6  2  12  4  10  4  10  8  6 };
OS = OPSCAL( 1,QUANTI,QUALIT );
```

The resulting vector **OS** has the following values:

$$\begin{bmatrix} 5 & 5 & 6 & 7 & 3 & 5 & 3 & 5 & 8 & 5 \end{bmatrix}.$$

The optimal scaling transformation result is said to "preserve the nominal measurement level of QUALIT" because wherever there was a QUALIT category c, there is now a result category label v. The transformation is least squares because the result element v is the mean of appropriate elements of QUANTI. This is Young's (1981) discrete-nominal transformation.

When QUALIT is at the ordinal level of measurement, the optimal scaling transformation result is a least-squares fit to QUANTI given the restriction that the ordinal structure of QUALIT must be preserved. This is done by determining blocks of elements of QUALIT so that if element i of QUALIT is in block b, then element i of the result is the mean of all those QUANTI elements corresponding to block b elements of QUALIT and so that the means are (weakly) in the same order as the elements of QUALIT. For example, consider these statements:

```
QUANTI = { 5   4   6   7   4   6   2   4 · 8   6 };
QUALIT = { 6   6   2  12   4  10   4  10   8   6 };
OS=OPSCAL(2,QUANTI,QUALIT);
```

The resulting vector **OS** has the following values:

$$\begin{bmatrix} 5 & 5 & 4 & 7 & 4 & 6 & 4 & 6 & 6 & 5 \end{bmatrix}.$$

This transformation preserves the ordinal measurement level of QUALIT because the elements of QUALIT and the result are (weakly) in the same order. It is least squares because the result elements are the means of appropriate elements of QUANTI. By comparing this result to the nominal one above, you see that categories whose means are incorrectly ordered have been merged together to form correctly ordered blocks. This is known as Kruskal's (1964) least-squares monotonic transformation.

Finally, consider these statements:

```
QUANTI = { 5   3   6   7   5   7   8   6   7   8 };
OS=OPSCAL(2,QUANTI);
```

These statements imply that

```
QUALIT = { 1   2   3   4   5   6   7   8   9  10 };
```

which means that the resulting vector has the values:

$$\begin{bmatrix} 4 & 4 & 6 & 6 & 6 & 7 & 7 & 7 & 7 & 8 \end{bmatrix}.$$

ORPOL Function: orthogonal polynomials

    ORPOL(*vector,maxdegree,weights*)
    ORPOL(*vector,maxdegree*)
    ORPOL(*vector*)

The ORPOL matrix function generates orthogonal polynomials.
    If *maxdegree* is omitted, IML uses the following default value:

      maxdegree (maximum degree polynomial to be computed)=min(n,20)

If *weights* is specified, *maxdegree* **must** be specified also.

The result is a column-orthonormal matrix **P** with the same number of rows as the vector and with *maxdegree*+1 columns:

$$P'*DIAG(weights)*P=I \quad .$$

The result is computed such that P[i,j] is the value of a polynomial of degree j−1 evaluated at the *i*th element of the vector.

Vector is an n x 1 (or 1 x n) vector of values over which the polynomials are to be defined. This argument must always be given.

Maxdegree specifies the maximum degree polynomial to be computed. Note that the number of columns in the computed result is 1+*maxdegree*, whether *maxdegree* is specified or the default value is used.

Weights specifies an n x 1 (or 1 x n) vector of nonnegative weights to be used in defining orthogonality: P'*DIAG(*weights*)*P=I. If you specify *weights*, you must specify *maxdegree* also. If *maxdegree* is not specified or is specified erroneously, the default weights (all weights=1) are used.

The maximum number of nonzero orthogonal polynomials (r) that can be computed from the vector and the weights is

r=the number of distinct values in the vector,
  ignoring any value associated with a zero
  weight.

The polynomial of maximum degree has degree=r−1. If the value of *maxdegree* exceeds r−1, then columns r +1, r +2, ..., *maxdegree* +1 of the result are set to zero. In this case,

$$P'*DIAG(weights)*P= \begin{matrix} I(r) & 0 \\ 0 & 0*J(maxdegree+1-r) \end{matrix}$$

See **Acknowledgments** for authorship of ORPOL.

PAUSE Statement: interrupt module execution

PAUSE;
PAUSE *charexpression*;

The PAUSE statement stops execution of a module, saves the calling chain so that execution can resume later (by a RESUME statement), prints a pause message that you can specify, and puts you in immediate mode so you can enter more statements.

You can specify an operand in the PAUSE statement to supply a message to be printed for the pause prompt. If no operand is specified, the default message, "paused in module XXX" is printed, where XXX is the name of the module containing the pause.

PAUSE should only be specified in modules. It generates an error message if executed in immediate mode.

PRINT Statement: print matrix values

PRINT *items*... ;

The PRINT statement prints the specified matrices.
Possible values for *items* are

name	name of matrix
(expression)	expression in parentheses, to print the results of the expression
"message"	message in quotes
,	to separate items, skip extra lines
/	to skip to a new page
[options]	options in brackets qualifying previous name

If a matrix row is too long for the print line, it is extended to the next line. The FW=*number* (field width) option of the RESET statement can be used to control the number of print positions for printing each matrix element.

The options below can appear in the PRINT statement. They are specified in brackets after the matrix name to which they apply.

FORMAT=*format*

specifies a format to use in printing the values of the matrix. For example,

```
PRINT X[FORMAT=5.3];
```

ROWNAME=*matrix*

specifies the name of a character matrix whose first *nrow* elements are to be used for the row labels of the matrix to be printed, where *nrow* is the number of rows in the matrix to be printed and where the scan to find the first *nrow* elements goes across row 1, then across row 2,..., and so forth through row *n*.

COLNAME=*matrix*

specifies the name of a character matrix whose first *ncol* elements are to be used for the column labels of the matrix to be printed, where *ncol* is the number of columns in the matrix to be printed and where the scan to find the first *nrow* elements goes across row 1, then across row 2,..., and so forth through row *n*.

For example, you can use this code to print a matrix called **X** in format 12.2 with columns headed 'AMOUNT' and 'NET PAY', and rows labeled 'DIV A' and 'DIV B'.

```
R=("DIV A"  "DIV B");
C=("AMOUNT" "NET PAY");

PRINT X[ROWNAME=R COLNAME=C FORMAT=12.2];
```

If there is not enough room to print all the matrices across together, then one or more matrices are printed out in the next group. If there is not enough room to print all the columns of a matrix across the page, then it will fold the columns, with the continuation lines identified by a colon(:).

PROBCHI Function: chi square distribution function

PROBCHI(*matrix,df*)
PROBCHI(*matrix,df,nc*)

PROBCHI is the scalar function returning for each element of the argument the probability that a random variable with a chi-square distribution falls below the value given. The second argument is for degrees of freedom. A third argument is optional and is a noncentrality parameter.

PROBF Function: F distribution function

> PROBF(*matrix,ndf,ddf*)
> PROBF(*matrix,ndf,ddf,nc*)

PROBF is the scalar function returning for each element of the argument matrix the probability that a random variable with an F distribution falls below the value given. The next two arguments are for degrees of freedom for numerator and denominator, respectively. A fourth argument may be given for a noncentrality parameter.

PROBIT Function: inverse normal distribution function

> PROBIT(*matrix*)

PROBIT is the scalar function returning for each element of the argument matrix the value such that a random variable with a normal distribution falls below the value with probability given by the argument.

PROBNORM Function: normal distribution function

> PROBNORM(*matrix*)

PROBNORM is the scalar function returning for each element of the argument matrix the probability that a random variable with a normal distribution falls below the value given.

PROBT Function: Student's t distribution function

> PROBT(*matrix,df*)
> PROBT(*matrix,df,nc*)

PROBT is the scalar function returning for each element of the argument matrix the probability that a random variable with a Student's t distribution falls below the value given. The second argument is for degrees of freedom, and the optional third argument is for the noncentrality parameter.

PURGE Statement: clean out deleted records

> PURGE;

This data processing statement is used to delete records previously marked for deletion. The PURGE operation effectively renumbers the records (observations) of the data set, closing the gaps created from deleted records.

PUT Statement: write data to external file

> PUT *items...* ;

The PUT statement writes to the file specified in the previously executed FILE statement, putting the values from IML variables. The statement is described in detail in "SAS/IML File Access."

The PUT statement is a sequence of positionals and record directives, variables, and formats. For example,

record directives
> start new records, specifically:

> /

>> writes out the current record and begins forming a new record.

> > *operand*

>> specifies to setup so that the next record written will start at the indicated byte position in the file (for RECFM=U files only). The operand is a literal number, a variable name, or an expression in parentheses.

positionals
> specifies the column on the record to which the PUT statement should go.

> @ *operand*

>> specifies to go to the indicated column, where operand is a literal number, a variable name, or an expression in parentheses. For example @30 means to go to column 30.

> + *operand*

>> specifies that the indicated number of columns are to be skipped. The operand is a literal number, a variable name, or an expression in parentheses.

putoperand
> specifies the value you want to put to the current position in the record. The operand can be either a variable name, a literal value, or an expression in parentheses. The put variable can be followed immediately by an output format specification.

format

> specifies an output format. These are of the form *w.d* or $*w*. for standard numeric and character formats where *w* is the width of the field and *d* is the decimal parameter, if any. They can also be a named format of the form: NAME*w.d* where NAME is the name of the format. If the width is unspecified, then a default width is used.

holding @-sign
> at the end of a PUT statement, instructs IML to put a hold on the current record so that IML can write more to the record with later PUT statements. Otherwise, IML automatically begins the next record for the next PUT statement.

QUIT Statement: exit from IML

QUIT;

Use the QUIT statement to exit IML. If a DATA or PROC statement is encountered, QUIT is implied. QUIT is executed immediately as it is seen; therefore, you cannot use QUIT as an executable statement; that is, as part of a module or conditional clause. (See the **ABORT Statement**).

RANK Function: ranking

RANK(*matrix*)

The RANK function creates a new matrix whose elements are the ranks of the corresponding elements of *matrix*. The ranks of tied values are assigned arbitrarily rather than averaged. (See the **RANKTIE Function**.) For

```
X={2 2 1 0 5};
```

RANK(X) produces the vector

$$\begin{bmatrix} 3 & 4 & 2 & 1 & 5 \end{bmatrix}$$.

This function can be used to sort a column vector:

```
B=A;
A[,RANK(A)]=B;
```

You can also use RANK to find anti-ranks of A:

```
R=RANK(A);
I=R;
I[,R]=1:NCOL(A);
```

RANKTIE Function: ranking with tie-averaging

RANKTIE(*matrix*)

The RANKTIE function creates a new matrix whose elements are the ranks of the corresponding elements of *matrix*. The ranks of tied values are averaged. For

```
X={2 2 1 0 5};
```

RANKTIE(X) produces the vector

$$\begin{array}{ccccc} & X & & & \\ 3.5 & 3.5 & 2 & 1 & 5 \end{array}$$

RANKTIE differs from the RANK function in that RANKTIE averages the ranks of tied values, whereas RANK arbitrarily breaks ties.

READ Statement: read records

READ <*range*> <VAR *operand*> <WHERE(*expression*)>;
READ <*range*> <VAR *operand*> <WHERE(*expression*)>
   INTO *name*<[ROWNAME=*name* COLNAME=*name*]>;

Use the READ statement to read variables or records from the current SAS data set into column matrices of the VAR *operand* or into the single matrix of the INTO clause. When the INTO clause is used, each variable in the VAR *operand* becomes a column of the target matrix and all variables in the VAR *operand* must be of the same type. If you specify no VAR *operand*, the default variables for the INTO clause are all numeric variables. Read all character variables into a target matrix by using VAR _CHAR_ as the operand.

You can specify ROWNAME and COLNAME matrices as part of the INTO clause. The COLNAME matrix specifies the name of a new character matrix to be created. This COLNAME matrix is created in addition to the target matrix of the INTO clause and contains variable names from the input data set corresponding to columns of the target matrix. The COLNAME matrix has dimensions 1 x *nvar*, where *nvar* is the number of variables contributing to the target matrix.

ROWNAME=*name* specifies the name of a character variable in the input data set. The values of this variable are put in a character matrix with the same name as the variable. This matrix has the dimensions *nobs* x 1, where *nobs* is the number of observations in the range of the READ statement.

For example,

```
READ ALL VAR{X Y};          reads all observations for the 2 variables
READ POINT 23;              reads all variables for observation 23
READ ALL
  VAR{NAME ADDR}
  WHERE(STATE="NJ");   reads name address of all from New Jersey
```

See the chapter "SAS/IML Data Processing" for further information.

REMOVE Function: discard elements

REMOVE(*matrix,indices*)

The REMOVE function returns as a row vector elements of the first argument, with elements corresponding to the indices in the second argument discarded and the gaps removed. The first argument is indexed in row-major order, as in subscripting, and the indices must be in the range 1 to the number of elements in the first argument. You can repeat the indices and can give them in any order. If all elements are removed, the result is a null matrix (zero rows and zero columns).

Thus,

```
A=REMOVE({5 6, 7 8}, 3);
```

removes the third element, giving:

$$A = \begin{bmatrix} 5 & 6 & 8 \end{bmatrix}$$

while

```
A=REMOVE({5 6 7 8}, {3 2 3 1});
```

causes all but the fourth element to be removed, giving

$$A = \begin{bmatrix} 8 \end{bmatrix}.$$

REMOVE Statement: remove matrix from storage

REMOVE *names;*

Use a REMOVE statement to remove a matrix from a library storage. See the chapter "SAS/IML Library Storage" and also the descriptions of LOAD, STORE, RESET and SHOW for related information.

RENAME Call: rename a SAS data set

```
CALL RENAME(libname,memname,newname);
CALL RENAME(memname,newname);
```

The RENAME function renames a SAS data set (or member) in the specified library. *libname* is a character scalar containing the SAS data library name. *memname* is a character scalar containing the old (current) name of the member to be renamed. *newname* is a character scalar containing the new name for the member.

REPEAT Function: repeating

```
REPEAT(matrix,nrow,ncol)
```

The REPEAT function creates a new matrix by repeating the values of the argument matrix *nrow*ncol* times, *nrow* times across the rows, and *ncol* times down the columns. For example,

```
X={1 2 , 3 4};
Y=REPEAT(X,2,3);
```

result in the matrix **Y**, repeating the **X** matrix twice down and three times across:

```
Y
1    2    1    2    1    2
3    4    3    4    3    4
1    2    1    2    1    2
3    4    3    4    3    4
```

REPLACE Statement: replace values in records, update an observation

```
REPLACE <range> <VAR operand> <WHERE(expression)>;
```

The REPLACE statement replaces the values of variables in a SAS data set with current values of the same variables from the work space. Use *range*, VAR, and WHERE operands to limit replacement to specific variables and observations. Replacement matrices should conform to the operation. REPLACE uses matrix elements in row order replacing the value on the *i*th observation with the *i*th matrix element. If there are more observations in *range* than matrix elements, REPLACE continues to use the last matrix element. For example, the statements

```
STATE="IL";
REPLACE ALL VAR{STATE} WHERE(STATE="ILL");
```

cause occurrences of "IL" to be replaced by "ILL" for the variable STATE.

The range, VAR, and WHERE clauses are all optional, and you can specify them in any order.

See the chapter "SAS/IML Data Processing" for further details.

RESET Statement: set options

```
RESET options;
```

The RESET statement sets processing options. The following are currently implemented options. Note that the prefix NO- turns off the feature. For options that take operands, the operand should be a literal, a name of a matrix containing the value, or an expression in parentheses.

PRINT
NOPRINT

    requests that IML print the results from assignment statements automatically.

LOG
NOLOG

    routes output to the log file rather than to the print file. This option is useful when running under the SAS Display Manager System. On the log, the results are interleaved with the statements and messages.

ALL
NOALL

    requests that IML print the results automatically, as in the PRINT option, but also print intermediate results.

FW=*number*

    sets field width for printing numeric values.

DETAILS
NODETAILS

    requests additional information from a variety of operations, such as when files are opened and closed.

FLOW
NOFLOW

    shows operations as executed and is used for debugging only.

NAME
NONAME

    prints matrix name with value for the PRINT statement.

CENTER
NOCENTER

    requests that printed output be centered on page.

LINESIZE=*n*

    specifies linesize for printing.

PAGESIZE=*n*

    specifies pagesize for printing.

STORAGE=*operand*

    specifies the file to be the current library storage for STORE and LOAD statements.

DEBUG
NODEBUG

    is used for debugging the IML system only.

DEFLIB=*operand*

    specifies the default libname for SAS data sets when no specific libname is given. This defaults to blanks, which in turn denotes 'USER' if a USER libname is set up, or 'WORK' if not.

SPACES=*n*

    specifies the number of spaces between printed results for the PRINT statement.

SPILL

specifies that a spill file be used for data processing applications that do not fit in memory.

CASE
NOCASE

specifies that the comparisons in data processing are case sensitive.

BREAK
NOBREAK

enables a break exit and escape mechanism.

RESUME Statement: resume execution

RESUME;

The RESUME statement allows you to continue execution from the line in the program where the most recent PAUSE statement was executed.

RETURN Statement: return to caller

RETURN;

The RETURN statement causes IML to return to the point in a program where a LINK statement was issued. If no LINK statement was issued, RETURN functions to exit a module. If not in a module, execution stops (as with a STOP statement), and IML looks for more statements to parse.

See the **LINK and RETURN Statements** above.

ROOT Function: Cholesky decomposition

ROOT(*matrix*)

The ROOT function performs the Cholesky decomposition of a matrix (for example, **A**) such that

$$U'U = A$$

where **U** is upper triangular. The matrix **A** must be symmetric and nonnegative definite.

ROWCAT Function: row concatenation without blank compression

ROWCAT(*matrix,rows,columns*)
ROWCAT(*matrix,rows*)
ROWCAT(*matrix*)

ROWCAT takes a character matrix or submatrix as argument and creates a new matrix with one column whose elements are the concatenation of all row elements into a single string. If the argument has *n* rows and *m* columns, the result will have *n* rows and 1 column. The element length of the result will be *m* times the element length of the argument. The optional rows and columns arguments may be used to select which rows and columns are concatenated. For example, if

```
B={"ABC"  "D "   "EF ",
   " GH"  " I "  " JK"};
```

then the statement

```
A=ROWCAT(B);
```

produces the new matrix

```
     A
ABCD  EF
GH I  JK
```

Quotation marks (") are needed only if you want to embed blanks or maintain uppercase and lowercase distinctions.
The form

ROWCAT(*matrix,rows,columns*)

returns the same result as

ROWCAT(*matrix[rows,columns]*)
while

ROWCAT(*matrix,rows*)

returns the same result as

ROWCAT(*matrix[rows,]*)   .

ROWCATC Function: row concatenation with blank compression

ROWCATC(*matrix,rows,columns*)
ROWCATC(*matrix,rows*)
ROWCATC(*matrix*)

Works the same way as ROWCAT except that blanks in element strings are moved to the end of the concatenation. For example, if

```
B=("ABC"  "D "  " EF ",
   " GH"  " I "  " JK");
```

then

```
A=ROWCATC(B);
```

produces the new matrix

```
   A
ABCDEF
GHIJK
```

Quotation marks (") are needed only if you want to embed blanks or maintain uppercase and lowercase distinctions.

RUN Statement

RUN;
RUN *name*;
RUN *name*(*arguments*,...);

The RUN statement requests IML to execute the statements that have been collected into a module.

See the section **Module Definition and Execution** in the chapter "SAS/IML Programming Statements" for further details.

SETDIF Function: set difference

SETDIF(*matrix1,matrix2*)

The SETDIF function returns as a row vector the sorted set (without duplicates) of all element values present in the first argument but not present in the second. If the resulting set is empty, SETDIF returns a null matrix (with zero rows and zero columns). The argument matrices and result may all be either character or numeric (but not mixed). For character matrices, the element length of the result is the same as the element length of the first matrix. Shorter elements in the second argument are padded with blanks for comparison purposes.

For example,

```
A={1 2 4 5};
B={3 4};
C=SETDIF(A,B);
```

gives the result

```
C={1 2 5};
```

SETIN Statement: select the current input data set

SETIN *SASdataset* <NOBS *name*> <POINT *operand*>;

The SETIN statement chooses the specified data set from among the data sets already opened for input by an EDIT or USE statement. This data set becomes the current data set for subsequent data management statements. NOBS is optional. If specified, NOBS returns the number of observations in the data set in the variable *name*. The POINT *operand* makes the specified observation the current one.

SETOUT Statement: select the current output data set

SETOUT *SASdataset* <NOBS *name*> <POINT *operand*>;

The SETOUT statement chooses the specified data set from among those data sets already opened for output by an EDIT statement. This data set becomes the current data set for subsequent data management statements. NOBS is optional. If specified, NOBS returns the number of observations currently in the data set in the scalar variable *name*. The POINT *operand* makes the specified observation the current one.

SHAPE Function: reshape and repeat values

SHAPE(*matrix,nrow*)
SHAPE(*matrix,nrow,ncol*)
SHAPE(*matrix,nrow,ncol,padvalue*)

The SHAPE function shapes a new matrix from a matrix with different dimensions; *nrow* specifies the number of rows, and *ncol* specifies the number of columns in the new matrix. The operator works for both numeric and character operands. The three ways of using the function are outlined below:

- If only *nrow* is specified, the number of columns is determined as the number of values in the object matrix divided by *nrow*. The number of values must be exactly divisible; otherwise, a conformability error is diagnosed.
- If both *nrow* and *ncol* are specified, but not *padvalue*, the result is obtained moving along the rows until the number of values is obtained. The operation cycles back to the beginning of the object matrix to get enough values.
- If *padvalue* is specified, the operation moves the values of the object matrix first and then fills in any extra positions in the result with the *padvalue*.

If *nrow* is specified as 0, the number of rows becomes the number of values divided by *ncol*.

Examples

```
R=SHAPE(12,3,4);
```

results in

$$R=\begin{bmatrix} 12 & 12 & 12 & 12 \\ 12 & 12 & 12 & 12 \\ 12 & 12 & 12 & 12 \end{bmatrix}$$

```
R=SHAPE(77,1,5);
```

results in

$$R=\begin{bmatrix} 77 & 77 & 77 & 77 & 77 \end{bmatrix} \qquad \text{(generating)}$$

```
R=SHAPE({1 2 ,
         3 4 ,
         5 6 },2);
```

results in

$$R=\begin{bmatrix} 1 & 2 & 3 \\ 4 & 5 & 6 \end{bmatrix} \qquad \text{(reshaping)}$$

```
R=SHAPE({99 31},3,3);
```

results in

$$R = \begin{bmatrix} 99 & 31 & 99 \\ 31 & 99 & 31 \\ 99 & 31 & 99 \end{bmatrix}$$ (cycling)

```
R=SHAPE({1 0 0 0 0},4,4);
```

results in

$$R = \begin{bmatrix} 1 & 0 & 0 & 0 \\ 0 & 1 & 0 & 0 \\ 0 & 0 & 1 & 0 \\ 0 & 0 & 0 & 1 \end{bmatrix}$$ (identity)

```
R=SHAPE({1 2,
         3 4}, 1,3);
```

results in

$$R = \begin{bmatrix} 1 & 2 & 3 \end{bmatrix}$$ (truncation)

```
R=SHAPE({9 8 7 6 5 4 3},3,3,0);
```

results in

$$R = \begin{bmatrix} 9 & 8 & 7 \\ 6 & 5 & 4 \\ 3 & 0 & 0 \end{bmatrix}$$ (padding with 0)

The following statements

```
Y={ 3 3 3 ,
    2 2 2 ,
    1 1 1 };
V=SHAPE(Y,9);
```

create the row vector **V**:

V

| 3 | 3 | 3 | 2 | 2 | 2 | 1 | 1 | 1 |

The statement

```
V=SHAPE(Y,1);
```

creates **V** as a column vector of nine elements.

SHOW Statement

SHOW *items*;

The SHOW statement requests that system information be printed. The following *items* are available:

OPTIONS   shows current settings of options (see the **RESET Statement**).

SPACE   shows the workspace size and how it is being used.

MODULES   shows the modules that have been defined.

ALL   shows all the information included by OPTIONS, SPACE, DATASETS, FILES, and MODULES.

STORAGE   shows the matrices in the current IML library storage on disk.

NAMES   shows attributes of all names having values.

ALLNAMES   behaves like NAMES, but also shows names without values.

DATASETS   shows all open SAS data sets.

CONTENTS   shows the names and attributes of the variables in the current SAS data set.

FILES   shows all open files.

WINDOWS   shows all active windows opened by WINDOW statements.

PAUSE   shows the paused modules that are pending resume.

name   shows attributes of the specified name. If the name of a matrix is one of the above keywords, then both the information for the keyword and the matrix are shown.

SIN Function: trigonometric sine

SIN(*matrix*)

SIN is the scalar function returning the sine of each element of the argument.

SOLVE Function: solve system of linear equations

SOLVE(*matrix1,matrix2*)

SOLVE solves the set of linear equations $AX=B$ for X. The A matrix must be square and nonsingular.

$X=$SOLVE(A,B) is equivalent to using the INV function as $X=$INV(A)*B. However, SOLVE is recommended over INV because it is more efficient and more accurate.

The solution method used is discussed in Forsythe and Moler (1967).

SORT Statement: sort a data set

SORT <DATA=>*fromdataset* <OUT=*todataset*> BY *variables*;

The SORT statement sorts the observations in a SAS data set by one or more variables, stores the resulting sorted observations in a new SAS data set or replaces the original. As opposed to all other IML data processing statements, it is **mandatory** that the data set to be sorted be closed prior to the execution of the SORT statement.

The SORT statement consists of the following clauses:

DATA=*SASdataset*

> names the SAS data set to be sorted. Note that the DATA= portion of the specification is optional. The *SASdataset* is specified as either *memname* or the compound *libname.memname*.

OUT=*SASdataset*

> specifies a name for the output data set. If this clause is omitted, the DATA= data set is sorted and the sorted version replaces the original data set.

BY *variables*

> specifies the variables to be sorted. A BY clause **must** be used with the SORT statement.
>
> SORT first arranges the observations in the order of the first variable in the BY clause; then it sorts the observations with a given value of the first variable by the second variable, and so forth. Every variable in the BY clause can be preceded by the keyword DESCENDING to denote that the variable that follows is to be sorted in descending order. Note that the SORT statement in IML always retains the same relative positions of the observations with identical BY variable values.

For example, the IML statement

```
SORT A.CLASS OUT=A.SCLASS BY DESCENDING AGE HEIGHT;
```

sorts the SAS data set CLASS by the variables AGE and HEIGHT, where AGE is sorted in descending order, and all observations with the same AGE value are rearranged by HEIGHT in ascending order. The output data set SCLASS contains the sorted observations.

Note that all the clauses of the SORT statement must be specified in the order given above.

SOUND Call: produce a tone

> CALL SOUND(*freq,dur*);
> CALL SOUND(*freq*);

The SOUND procedure generates a tone using *freq* for frequency (in hertz) and *dur* for duration (in seconds). Matrices may be specified for frequency and duration to produce multiple tones, but if both arguments are nonscalar, then the number of elements must match. The duration argument is optional and defaults to 0.25 (one quarter second).

For example,

```
NOTES=400 # (2 ## DO(0, 1, 1/12));
 CALL SOUND(NOTES 0.2);
```

produces tones from an ascending musical scale, all with a duration of 0.2 seconds.

SQRSYM Function: convert symmetric matrix to square matrix

SQRSYM(*matrix*)

The SQRSYM function takes a matrix like those generated by SYMSQR and transforms it back into a square matrix. The elements of the argument are unpacked into the lower triangle of the result and reflected across the diagonal into the upper triangle.

For example,

```
SQR=SQRSYM(SYMSQR({1 2, 3 4}));
```

which is the same as

```
SQR=SQRSYM({1, 3, 4});
```

produces

$$SQR = \begin{bmatrix} 1 & 3 \\ 3 & 4 \end{bmatrix}.$$

SQRT Function: square root

SQRT(*matrix*)

SQRT is the scalar function returning the positive square roots of each element of the argument.

SSQ Function: sum of squares of all elements

SSQ(*matrix1,matrix2,...matrixn*)

The SSQ function returns as a single numeric value the (uncorrected) sum of squares for all the elements of all arguments. You can specify as many as 15 numeric argument matrices.

The SSQ function checks for missing arguments and does not include them in the accumulation. If all arguments are missing, the result is 0.

START and FINISH Statements

START;
START *name*;
START *name* (*argument,argument,...*);
statements;
FINISH;

The START statement instructs IML to enter a module collect mode to collect the statements of a module rather than execute them immediately. The FINISH statement signals the end of a module. See the section **Module Definition and Execution** in the chapter "SAS/IML Programming Statements" for further information.

STOP Statement

STOP;

The STOP statement stops the IML program, and no further matrix statements are executed. However, IML continues to execute if more statements are entered. See the **RETURN** and **ABORT Statements**.

If IML execution was interrupted by a PAUSE statement or by a break, the STOP statement clears all the paused states and returns to true immediate mode.

STORE Statement: store matrices on disk storage

    STORE;
    STORE names;

The STORE statement stores matrix values on the disk library. If you do not name any matrices, all matrices are stored. If you want to store some matrices but not others, you must list the names of the matrices to be stored.

SUBSTR Function: substring

    SUBSTR(matrix,position,length)
    SUBSTR(matrix,position)

The SUBSTR function takes a character matrix as an argument along with starting *position*(s) and *length*(s) and produces a character matrix with the same dimensions as the argument. Elements of the result matrix are substrings of the corresponding argument elements. Each substring is constructed using the starting *position* supplied. If a *length* is supplied, this length is the length of the substring. If no *length* is supplied, the remainder of the argument string is included in the substring.

Position and *length* can be scalars or numeric matrices. If *position* or *length* is a matrix, its dimensions must be the same as the dimensions of the argument matrix or submatrix. If either of these second and third arguments is a matrix, its values are applied to the substringing of the corresponding elements of the first argument. If *length* is supplied, the element length of the result is MAX(*length*); otherwise, the element length of the result is

$$NLENG(matrix) - MIN(position) + 1 \quad .$$

The statements

    B={abc def ghi, jkl mno pqr};
    A=SUBSTR(B,3,2);

return the result

                        A
                    C   F   I
                    L   O   R

SUM Function: sum of all elements

    SUM(matrix1,matrix2,...matrixn)

SUM returns as a single numeric value the sum of all the elements in all arguments. There can be as many as 15 argument matrices. The SUM function checks for missing values and does not include them in the accumulation. It returns zero if all values are missing.

SUMMARY Statement: summaries of SAS data sets

SUMMARY <CLASS *operand*>
    <VAR *operand*>
    <WEIGHT *operand*>
    <STAT *operand*>
    <OPT *operand*>
    <WHERE (*expression*)>;

The SUMMARY statement in IML computes statistics for numeric variables for an entire data set or a subset of observations in the data set. The statistics can be stratified by the use of class variables. The computed statistics are displayed in tabular form and can be optionally saved in matrices. Like most other IML data processing statements, the SUMMARY statement works on the current data set.

The SUMMARY statement is built from the clauses described below. The operands used by most clauses take either a matrix literal value, the name of a matrix, or an expression yielding a matrix value.

CLASS *operand*

> specifies the variables on the current input SAS data set to be used to group the summaries. The operand is a character value containing the names of the variables. For example,

>> `SUMMARY CLASS {AGE SEX};`

> Both numeric and character variables can be used as class variables.

VAR *operand* or _NUM_

> requests statistics for a set of numeric variables from the current input data set. The *operand* is a character matrix value containing the names of the variables. Also, the special keyword _NUM_ can be used (without the keyword VAR) to specify all numeric variables. If the VAR clause is missing, SUMMARY produces only the number of observations in each subgroup.

WEIGHT *operand*

> specifies a character value containing the name of a numeric variable in the current data set whose values are to be used to weight each observation. Only one variable can be specified.

STAT *operand*

> explicitly requests certain statistics to be computed. The operand is a character value containing the requested statistics. For example, to get the mean and standard deviation, specify

>> `SUMMARY STAT{MEAN STD};`

> Below is a list of the keywords that can be specified as the STAT *operand*:

> N

>> requests that IML compute the number of observations in the subgroup used in the computation of the various statistics for the corresponding analysis variable.

> NMISS

>> requests that IML compute the number of observations in the subgroup having missing values for the analysis variable.

MIN

> requests that IML compute the minimum value.

MAX

> requests that IML compute the maximum value.

SUM

> requests that IML compute the sum.

SUMWGT

> requests that IML compute the sum of the WEIGHT variable values, if WEIGHT is specified; otherwise, IML computes the number of observations used in the computation of statistics.

USS

> requests that IML compute the uncorrected sum of squares.

MEAN

> requests that IML compute the mean.

CSS

> requests that IML compute the corrected sum of squares.

VAR

> requests that IML compute the variance.

STD

> requests that IML compute the standard deviation.

When the STAT clause is omitted, SUMMARY computes these statistics for each variable in the VAR clause:

> MIN   is the MINIMUM VALUE of the variable.
>
> MAX   is the MAXIMUM VALUE of the variable.
>
> MEAN   is the MEAN or average of the variable.
>
> STD   is the STANDARD DEVIATION of the variable.

Note that NOBS, the number of observations in each CLASS group, is always given.

OPT *operand*

> sets the PRINT or NOPRINT, SAVE or NOSAVE options. NOPRINT suppresses the printing of the results from the SUMMARY statement. SAVE requests that SUMMARY save the resultant statistics in matrices.
>
> When the SAVE option is set, SUMMARY creates a class vector for each class variable, a statistic matrix for each analysis variable, and a column vector named _NOBS_. The class vectors are named by the corresponding class variable and have an equal number of rows. There are as many rows as there are subgroups defined by the interaction of all class variables. The statistics matrices are named by the corresponding analysis variable. Each column of the statistic matrix corresponds to a statistic requested, and each row corresponds to the statistics of the subgroup defined by the class variables. If no class variable has been specified, each statistic matrix will have one row, containing the statistics of the entire population. The _NOBS_ vector contains the number of observations for each subgroup.
>
> The default OPT *operand* is PRINT NOSAVE.

WHERE *expression*

> specifies the subset of the current data set for SUMMARY to process. See the chapter "SAS/IML Data Processing" for further information.

For example, suppose the current data set has the variables SEX, AGE, HEIGHT, WEIGHT. The statement

```
SUMMARY CLASS (SEX) VAR (HEIGHT WEIGHT AGE);
```

produces the following output:

SEX	NOBS	VARIABLE	MIN	MAX	MEAN	STD
F	9	HEIGHT	51.3	66.5	60.588888889	5.0183275213
		WEIGHT	50.5	112.5	90.111111111	19.38391372
		AGE	11	15	13.222222222	1.3944333776
M	10	HEIGHT	57.3	72	63.91	4.9379370411
		WEIGHT	83	150	108.95	22.727186363
		AGE	11	16	13.4	1.6465452047
All	19	HEIGHT	51.3	72	62.336842105	5.1270752466
		WEIGHT	50.5	150	100.02631579	22.773933494
		AGE	11	16	13.315789474	1.4926721594

SVD CALL: singular value decomposition

CALL SVD(U,Q,V,A);

The SVD subroutine decomposes a real $m \times n$ matrix A (where $m >= n$) into the form

$$A = U * diag(Q) * V'$$

where

$$U'U = V'V = VV' = I_n$$

and Q contains the singular values. U is $m \times n$, Q is $n \times 1$, and V is $n \times n$.

When $m >= n$, U consists of the orthonormal eigenvectors of AA' and V consists of the eigenvectors of $A'A$. Q contains the square roots of the eigenvalues of $A'A$ and AA', except for some zeros.

If $m < n$, a corresponding decomposition is done where U and V switch roles:

$$A = U * diag(Q) * V'$$

but

$$U'U = UU' = V'V = I_m .$$

For information about the method used in SVD, see Wilkinson and Reinsch (1971).

To sort the singular values, use

```
CALL SVD (U,Q,V,A);
R=RANK(Q);
TEMP=U; U[,R]=TEMP;
TEMP=Q; Q[R,]=TEMP;
TEMP=V; V[,R]=TEMP;
```

SWEEP Function: sweep operator

SWEEP(*matrix,indexvector*)

The SWEEP function sweeps *matrix* on the pivots indicated in *indexvector* to produce a new matrix. The values of the index vector must be less than or equal to the number of rows or the number of columns in *matrix,* whichever is smaller.

For example, suppose that **A** is partitioned into

$$\begin{bmatrix} R & S \\ T & U \end{bmatrix}$$

such that

R is q x q, **U** is (m−q) x (n−q)   .

Let

I = 1:q;   which is: 1 2 3 ... q

then

S=SWEEP(A,I)

becomes

$$\begin{bmatrix} R^{-1} & R^{-1}S \\ -TR^{-1} & U-TR^{-1}S \end{bmatrix}$$.

The index vector can be omitted. In this case, the function sweeps the matrix on all pivots on the main diagonal 1:MIN(*nrow,ncol*).

The SWEEP function has sequential and reversibility properties when the submatrix swept is positive definite. For example,

```
SWEEP(SWEEP(A,1),2)=SWEEP(A,{1 2})
SWEEP(SWEEP(A,I),I)=A
```

See Beaton (1964) for more information about these properties.

To use SWEEP for regression, suppose the matrix **A** contains

$$\begin{bmatrix} X'X & X'Y \\ Y'X & Y'Y \end{bmatrix}$$

where **X'X** is k x k.

Then **B**=SWEEP(**A**,1...k) contains

$$\begin{bmatrix} (X'X)^{-1} & (X'X)^{-1}X'Y \\ -Y'X(X'X)^{-1} & Y'(I-X(X'X)^{-1}X')Y \end{bmatrix} \quad .$$

The partitions of **B** form the beta values, SSE, and a matrix proportional to the covariance of the beta values for the least-squares estimates of **B** in the linear model:

$$Y = X B + \varepsilon \quad .$$

If any pivot becomes very close to zero ($<=1E^{-12}$), t he row and column for that pivot are zeroed. See Goodnight (1979) for more information.

SYMSQR Function: convert square matrix to symmetric matrix

SYMSQR(*matrix*)

The SYMSQR function takes a square numeric matrix (size n x n) and compacts the elements from the lower triangle into a column vector ($n * (n + 1) / 2$ rows). The matrix is not checked for actual symmetry. Therefore,

```
SYM=SYMSQR({1 2, 3 4});
```

sets

$$SYM = \begin{bmatrix} 1 \\ 3 \\ 4 \end{bmatrix} \quad .$$

Note that the 2 is lost since it is only present in the upper triangle.

TAN Function: trigonometric tangent

TAN(*angle*)

The trigonometric tangent accepts angles in radians and returns the tangent function, which has an infinite range. If the argument is a matrix of values, the function returns a matrix of elementwise tangent results.

TRACE Function: sum of diagonal elements

TRACE(*matrix*)

TRACE produces a single numeric value that is the sum of the diagonal elements of matrix.

UNIFORM Function: pseudo-random uniform deviate

UNIFORM(*seed*)

UNIFORM is a scalar function returning one or more pseudo-random numbers with a uniform distribution over the interval 0 to 1. The UNIFORM function returns a matrix with the same dimensions as the argument. The first argument on the first call is used for the seed—or if that is zero, the system clock is used for the seed.

UNION Function: set union

UNION(*matrix1,matrix2,...matrixn*)

The UNION function returns as a row vector the sorted set (without duplicates) which is the union of the element values present in its arguments. There can be as many as 15 arguments, which can be character or numeric. For character arguments, the element length of the result is the longest element length of the arguments. Shorter character elements are padded with blanks. This function is identical to the UNIQUE function. For example,

```
A={1 2 4 5};
B={3 4};
C=UNION(A,B);
```

sets

$$C = \begin{bmatrix} 1 & 2 & 3 & 4 & 5 \end{bmatrix} .$$

UNIQUE Function: sort and remove duplicates

UNIQUE(*matrix1,matrix2,...matrixn*)

The UNIQUE function returns as a row vector the sorted set (without duplicates) of all the element values present in its arguments. The arguments are numeric or character, and there can be as many as 15 specified. This function is identical to the UNION function above, which includes an example.

USE Statement: open SAS data set for reading

USE *SASdataset* <*range*> <VAR *operand*> <WHERE(*expression*)>;

If the data set has not already been opened, the USE statement opens the data set. The statement also makes this the "current" data set so that subsequent statements act on it. USE can also define the variables matrix and the selection criteria that are used to control access.

The *range*, VAR, and WHERE clauses are optional, and you can specify them in any order.

See the chapter "SAS/IML Data Processing" for further information.

VALSET Call: indirect assignment

CALL VALSET(*char_scalar,argument*);

The VALSET call expects a single character string argument containing the name of a matrix. VALSET looks up the matrix and moves the value of the second argument to this matrix. For example,

```
B="A";
CALL VALSET(B,99);
```

finds that the value of the argument **B** is **A** and then looks up **A** and copies the value 99 to **A**, the indirect result. The previous value of the indirect result would be freed.

VALUE Function: indirect reference

VALUE(*char_scalar*)

The VALUE function expects a single character string argument containing the name of a matrix. VALUE looks up the matrix and moves its value to the result. For example, the statements

```
A={ 1 2 3 };
B="A";
C=VALUE(B);
```

find that the value of the argument **B** is **A** and then look up **A** and copy the value {1 2 3} to **C**, the result.

VECDIAG Function: vector from diagonal

VECDIAG(*squarematrix*)

VECDIAG creates a column vector whose elements are the main diagonal elements of *squarematrix*.

WINDOW Statement: open a display window

WINDOW <CLOSE=>*windowname* <*windowoptions*>
<GROUP=*groupname fieldspecs*>... ;

The window statement defines a window on the display screen and can include a number of fields. The DISPLAY statement actually writes values to the window. The fields that can be specified in the WINDOW statement are

windowname
> specifies a 1-8 character name for the window. This name is displayed in the upper-left border of the window.

CLOSE=*windowname*
> closes the window.

windowoptions
> controls the size, position, and other attributes of the window. The attributes can also be changed interactively with window commands such as WGROW, WDEF, WSHRINK, COLOR. The window options are

> ROWS=*operand*
>> determines the starting number of rows of the window. The default is 23 rows. *Operand* is either a literal number, the name of a variable containing the number, or an expression in parentheses yielding the number.

> COLUMNS=*operand*
>> specifies the starting number of columns of the window. The default is 78 columns. *Operand* is either a literal number, a variable name, or an expression in parentheses.

> IROW=*operand*
>> specifies the initial starting row position of the window on the display screen. The default is row 1. *Operand* is either a literal number, a variable name, or an expression in parentheses.

ICOLUMN=*operand*

specifies the initial starting column position of the window on the display screen. The default is column 1. *Operand* is either a literal number, a variable name, or an expression in parentheses.

COLOR=*operand*

specifies the background color for the window. The default color is BLACK. *Operand* is either a quoted character literal, a name, or an operand. The valid values are "WHITE", "BLACK", "GREEN", "MAGENTA", "RED", "YELLOW", "CYAN", "GRAY", and "BLUE".

CMNDLINE=*name*

specifies the name of a variable in which the command line entered by the user will be stored.

MSGLINE=*operand*

specifies the message to be displayed on the standard message line when the window is made active. *Operand* is almost always the name of a variable, but a character literal can be used.

GROUP=*groupname*

starts a repeating sequence of groups of fields defined for the window. The *groupname* specification is a 1-8 character name used to identify a group of fields on a later DISPLAY statement.

fieldspecs

are a sequence of field specifications made up of positionals, field operands, formats, and options. These are described in the following section.

Field specifications Both the WINDOW and DISPLAY statements allow field specifications, which have the syntax:

   <*positionals...*> *fieldoperand* <*format*> <*field options...*>

positionals

are directives determining the position on the screen to begin the field. There are four kinds of positionals; any number of positionals are allowed for each field operand.

operand

specifies the row position; that is, it moves the current position to column 1 of the specified line. The *operand* is either a number, a name, or an expression in parentheses.

/

specifies that the current position move to column 1 of the next row.

@ *operand*

specifies the column position. The *operand* is either a number, a name, or an expression in parentheses. The @ directive should come after the # position if # is specified.

+ *operand*

specifies a skip of columns. The *operand* is either a number, a name, or an expression in parentheses.

fieldoperand

> a character literal in quotes or the name of a variable that specifies what is to go in the field.

format

> the format used for display, the value, and the informat applied to entered values. If no format is specified, then the standard numeric or character format is used.

fieldoptions

> specify the attributes of the field as follows:
>
> PROTECT=YES
> P=YES
>
> > specifies that the field is protected; that is, you cannot enter values in the field. If the field operand is a literal, it is already protected.
>
> COLOR=*operand*
>
> > specifies the color of the field. The default color is "BLUE". The *operand* is a literal character value in quotes, a variable name, or an expression in parentheses.The colors available are: "WHITE", "BLACK", "GREEN", "MAGENTA", "RED", "YELLOW", "CYAN", "GRAY", and "BLUE". Note that the color specification is different from that of the corresponding DATA step value because it is an operand rather than a name without quotes.

XSECT Function: set intersection

XSECT(*matrix1,matrix2,...matrixn*)

The XSECT function returns as a row vector the sorted set (without duplicates) of the element values that are present in all of its arguments. This set is the intersection of the sets of values in its argument matrices. When the intersection is empty, XSECT returns a null matrix (zero rows and zero columns). There can be as many as 15 arguments, which must all be either character or numeric. For characters, the element length of the result is the same as the shortest of the element lengths of the arguments. For sorting purposes, shorter elements are padded with blanks.

For example,

```
A={1 2 4 5};
B={3 4};
C=XSECT(A,B);
```

returns

$$C = \begin{bmatrix} 4 \end{bmatrix} .$$

APPENDICES

SAS/IML™ Software Compared to
PROC MATRIX

Changes and Enhancements to SAS/IML™
Software for Version 6

SAS/IML™ Quick Reference

The MATRIX/IML™ Translator Procedure

APPENDICES

SAS/IML™ Software Compared to PROC MATRIX

This appendix introduces PROC IML to those who already know PROC MATRIX.

PROC MATRIX is an older SAS procedure that implemented a matrix programming language. PROC MATRIX is becoming obsolete due to the development of IML, a much more refined and capable procedure. PROC MATRIX still works in Version 5 SAS on IBM OS environments, and you can still obtain documentation for PROC MATRIX in the form of technical report P-135, which is an extract of the *SAS User's Guide: Statistics* documentation for PROC MATRIX.

PROC IML is like PROC MATRIX in many ways. The following items highlight the differences.

1. Literals

IML literals with more than one element must be enclosed with braces. For example,

```
A={1 2 3,
   4 5 6};
```

Rows are separated by commas rather than slashes. These changes correct several problems. The sign change and subtract operators can no longer be confused with signs in numeric literals. For example,

```
Y=X**2-1;
```

Also, the slash can now be used for division. A −7 generates a change-sign operator on seven rather than a negative 7.

2. Character Matrices and Literals

A matrix can now be character valued. Each element can be a string up to 32767 bytes long. Each element of a matrix is the same size. Literals are given in single or double quotes; for example, A="coffee". Literals with several elements are enclosed in brackets ([ ]) like numeric matrix literals. Strings inside the brackets need not be enclosed in quotes if they are valid names and if you do not mind them being translated to uppercase.

These conventions address several problems in PROC MATRIX: character-valued matrices were fixed in size and they were not recognized by most operations as character-valued. For example, the PRINT command did not know a matrix was character-valued unless a character format was used.

3. **Subscripts are specified differently.**
Subscripts are written using brackets as a postfix operator with one or two arguments enclosed in [ ]. Below are several examples:

`A=B[row,column];`	right-hand-side selection
`A[row,column]=B;`	left-hand-side insertion
`A=B[elements];`	right-hand-side selection
`A[elements]=B;`	left-hand-side insertion

Either argument can be left empty to signify all rows or columns. Right-side subscripts can be reduction operators.

This change is needed to eliminate the old ambiguity between subscripted matrices and functions with arguments. The old rule of first use does not work now that resolution is delayed until after parsing.

The subscript operator for MEAN is a colon (:) in IML, not a period (.). This is necessary because periods are parsed as missing values.

Single subscripts are allowed. They refer to the matrix element in row-major order. For vectors with only one row or column, this accesses the expected element. For example,

```
A={ 1 2 3,
    4 5 6 };
```

`B=A[5];`   yields the value $\begin{bmatrix} 5 \end{bmatrix}$

`C=A[{2 5 1 }];` yields the vector $\begin{bmatrix} 2 \\ 5 \\ 1 \end{bmatrix}$

`A[5]=10;`   is allowed.

4. **Certain special character operators have changed.**
Under IML, division is now / rather than #/. The rarely used horizontal direct product operator @ | has been implemented as the HDIR function. The transpose operator is a backquote (`) rather than '.

5. **Certain commands have been dropped.**
Under IML, the EIGEN, SVD, and GS commands have been converted into calls. For example,

```
CALL EIGEN(M,E,A);
```

The GSORTH call is available in Version 5, but not yet in Version 6.

6. **NOTE is gone, PRINT is enhanced.**
Under IML, replace NOTE commands with PRINT commands. PRINT accepts quoted strings and commas, in addition to matrix names.

Separate each PRINT argument from the next with a comma unless you mean for them to print side-by-side. Extra commas cause extra spacing lines, and slashes (/) force a new page. PRINT also affords more control over labeling and formatting printed matrices.

7. **Error diagnostics are different**.
   In IML, syntax errors are reported with the tokens that were expected by the grammar. Sometimes this can be misleading.

8. **I/O to SAS data sets is different**.
   In IML, many new commands are provided for SAS data set I/O. FETCH has been implemented as

   READ INTO *matrixname*

   and OUTPUT has been implemented as

   APPEND FROM *matrixname*

   in order to be consistent with the new data management commands.

9. **SHAPE has changed.**
   In IML, the second argument of SHAPE is the number of rows, not columns. Columns is an optional third argument.

Changes and Enhancements to SAS/IML™ Software for Version 6

There are a number of differences between Version 6 SAS/IML, which runs on PCs, and Version 5 SAS/IML, which runs on mainframes. Many of these differences are enhancements, but a few are limitations. These differences are summarized below:

subscripts
Version 6 IML does not support the parenthesis-vertical-bar substitution for square brackets used primarily in subscripts. Square brackets are used exclusively. For example,

Version 5: `X=A(|I|);`

Version 6: `X=A[I];`

literals
Version 6 IML has a repetition feature for matrix literals in braces. It also allows certain special characters inside braces.

graphics
Version 6 IML does not support any of the graphics functions supported by Version 5 IML.

data processing
Version 6 IML supports indexing of SAS data sets by one or more key variables.

PAUSE and RESUME statements
In Version 6 IML, you can use a PAUSE statement to suspend execution, which you can resume later with a RESUME statement.

file access
Version 6 IML has the following statements for external file access: INFILE, FILE, INPUT, PUT, and CLOSEFILE.

RUN statement
Version 6 does not support the *keyword=* arguments.

new commands
Version 6 IML supports several new commands. These include SORT and SUMMARY.

interrupts

> In Version 6 IML, you can break out of execution.

printing

> In Version 6 IML, the PRINT command does not make default row and column names. (Version 5 IML made names like ROW1 and COL1.) The examples in this book may show these labels, even though they do not appear if the programs are run under Version 6.

display features

> Version 6 IML has display features for full-screen data entry or menuing, as implemented in the WINDOW and DISPLAY statements.

new functions

> Version 6 IML supports several new functions. These include BYTE, CUSUM, DO, INSERT, REMOVE, SETDIF, SOUND, SQRSYM, SYMSQR, UNION, UNIQUE, and XSECT.

omitted functions

> Version 6 IML does not support the following functions: ARMACOV, ARMALIK, BRANKS, BTRAN, COVLAG, CVEXHULL, ECHELON, FFT, HANKEL, HERMITE, IFFT, INVUPDT, IPF, MARG, PARSE, PGRAF, PRODUCT, RATIO, SPLINE, STORAGE, SUBSTR(pseudo-variable), TOEPLITZ, and XMULT. Note that these are the more specialized technical functions.

new options

> The following new options are available under Version 6 IML: ALL, CENTER, DEFLIB=, LINESIZE, NAME, and PAGESIZE.

new SHOW keywords

> The following new SHOW keywords are available under Version 6 IML: ALLNAMES, FILES, PAUSE, WINDOWS.

miscellaneous

> In Version 6 IML, you can specify a DATA clause in the DO statement.

SAS/IML™ Quick Reference

Table A3.1 Operators

Operation	Symbol	Syntax type	Data type
sign reverse	−	prefix	num
addition	+	infix	num
subtraction	−	infix	num
index creation	:	infix	num
matrix multiplication	*	infix	num
element multiplication	#	infix	num
direct product	@	infix	num
matrix power	**	infix	num
element power	##	infix	num
division	/	infix	num
horizontal concatenation	||	infix	both
vertical concatenation	//	infix	both
element maximum	<>	infix	both
element minimum	><	infix	both

(*continued on next page*)

Table A3.1   (continued)

Operation	Symbol	Syntax type	Data type
and	&	infix	num
or	|	infix	num
not	^	prefix	num
less than	<	infix	both
greater than	>	infix	both
equal to	=	infix	both
less or equal	<=	infix	both
greater or equal	>=	infix	both
not equal	^=	infix	both
transpose	`	postfix	both
subscript	[ ]	postfix	both

Table A3.2   Operator Precedence

Group I (highest priority)

^   `   subscripts   −(prefix)   ##   **

Group II

*   #   <>   ><   /   @

Group III

+   −

Group IV

|| //   :

Group V

<   <=   >   >=   =   ^=

Group VI

&

Group VII (lowest priority)

|

Table A3.3 Subscript Reduction Operators

+	addition
#	multiplication
<>	maximum
><	minimum
<:>	index of maximum
>:<	index of minimum
:	mean
##	sum of squares

Table A3.4 Functions

Function	Example	Arg type
all elements nonzero?	B=ALL(A);	num
any elements nonzero?	I=ANY(A);	num
combine diagonally	C=BLOCK(A,B);	num
get ASCII byte by number	CHAR=BYTE(*number*);	char
change substrings	CALL CHANGE(*matrix,old,new*);	char
numeric to character	C=CHAR(NUM,W,D)	num
element concatenation	C=CONCAT(A,B);	char
contents of data set	R=CONTENTS(*lib,mem*);	char
character reshaping	R=CSHAPE(*matrix,nrow,ncol,size<,pad>*);	char
cumulative sum	C=CUSUM(*matrix*);	num
find SAS data sets	R=DATASETS(*libname*);	char
delete a data set	CALL DELETE(*lib,mem*);	
create design matrix	X=DESIGN(A);	num
create full-rank design matrix	X=DESIGNF(A);	num
determinant	D=DET(A);	num
diagonal	D=DIAG(A);	num
index generation	I=DO(*i1,i2,inc*);	num
eigenvalues and vectors	CALL EIGEN(M,E,A);	num
eigenvalues	M=EIGVAL(A);	num
generalized inverse	G=GINV(A);	num
Cholesky root	U=HALF(A);	num

(*continued on next page*)

Table A3.4   (continued)

Function	Example	Arg type
horizontal direct product	`H=HDIR(A,B);`	num
identity matrix	`B=I(A);`	num
insert a new element	`R=INSERT(X,Y,ROW,COL);`	both
matrix inverse	`I=INV(A);`	num
matrix of identical values	`B=J(NR,NC,VAL);`	num
length of longest string	`B=LENGTH(A);`	char
location of nonzeros	`B=LOC(A);`	num
maximum value	`B=MAX(A);`	both
minimum value	`B=MIN(A);`	both
name of arguments	`N=NAME(A,...);`	both
number of columns	`N=NCOL(A);`	both
length of element	`B=NLENG(A);`	both
number or rows	`K=NROW(A);`	both
character to numeric	`N=NUM(A);`	char
optimal scaling	`OPSCAL(MLEVEL,QUANTI);`	num
orthogonal polynomials	`A=ORPOL(X,MD,W);`	num
ranking values	`R=RANK(A);`	num
ranking with ties averaged	`R=RANKTIE(X);`	num
remove element	`R=REMOVE(matrix,indices);`	both
rename a SAS data set	`CALL RENAME(lib,mem,new);`	char
repeat a matrix	`R=REPEAT(matrix,rows,cols);`	num
Cholesky decomposition	`U=ROOT(A);`	num
row concatenation	`R=ROWCATB(A,B);`	char
row concatenation	`R=ROWCATC(A,B);`	char

(continued on next page)

Table A3.4 (continued)

Function	Example	Arg type
set difference	D=SETDIF(A,B);	both
reshape	B=SHAPE(A,NROW,NCOL);	both
solve linear system	X=SOLVE(A,C);	num
produce tone	CALL SOUND(*freq<,dur>*);	num
convert symmetric to square	SQR=SQRSYM(SYM);	char
sum of squares	S=SSQ(A);	num
substring	A=SUBSTR(B,START,LEN);	char
sum	S=SUM(A);	num
singular value decomp	CALL SVD(U,M,V,A);	num
sweep	B=SWEEP(A,1:5);	num
convert square to symmetric	SYM=SYMSQR(*sqr*);	num
trace	T=TRACE(X);	num
union set operator	U=UNION(*matrix<,...>*);	both
form unique set, union	U=UNIQUE(*matrix<,...>*);	both
value assignment	*call* VALSET(A,B);	char
value lookup	V=VALUE(A);	char
diagonal to vector	V=VECDIAG(A);	num
set intersection	R=XSECT(A,B);	both

Table A3.5   Scalar Functions

Function	Usage
absolute value	`A=ABS(X);`
arc-cosine	`S=ARCOS(X);`
arc-sine	`S=ARSIN(X);`
arc-tangent	`S=ATAN(X);`
cosine	`S=COS(X);`
exponential	`B=EXP(X);`
integer value (truncation)	`I=INT(X);`
natural logarithm	`Y=LOG(X);`
modulo (remainder)	`Y=MOD(X,D);`
chi-square distribution	`P=PROBCHI(X,DF,NC);`
F distribution	`P=PROBF(X,NDF,DDF,NC);`
inverse normal distribution	`P=PROBIT(X);`
normal distribution	`P=PROBNORM(X);`
t distribution	`P=PROBT(X,DF,NC);`
normal random number	`N=NORMAL(SEED);`
sine	`S=SIN(X);`
square root	`S=SQRT(X);`
tangent	`S=TAN(X);`
uniform random number	`U=UNIFORM(SEED);`

Table A3.6   General Purpose Commands

Command	Example
module definition finish	`FINISH;`
free storage	`FREE names;`
storage retrieve	`LOAD names;`
storage remove	`REMOVE names;`
set options	`RESET options;`
print matrices	`PRINT names messages;`
exit from IML	`QUIT;`
module execute	`RUN name arguments;`
show status	`SHOW items;`
module definition start	`START name arguments;`
storage store	`STORE names;`
associates print attributes	`MATTRIB name;`

Table A3.7 Control Statements

IF-THEN/ELSE	conditional statements
DO-END	grouping
iterative DO-END	iteration
GOTO	transfer control
LINK	goto with return link
RETURN	return to caller
STOP	stop execution
ABORT	stop execution and exit IML
PAUSE	pause execution
RESUME	resume from pause

Table A3.8 RESET Options

Option	Effect
PRINT	prints all results automatically.
NAME	controls printing of matrix name and default row and column names.
FLOW	traces flow of execution with messages.
DETAILS	causes more details to be shown.
FW=	specifies field width for printing matrices.
STORAGE=	specifies the matrix library storage.
DEFLIB=	is the default libname for SAS data sets.
LOG	routes output to log rather than output scroll.
DEBUG	is for IML debugging only.
ALL	prints intermediate results automatically.
CENTER	centers output.
LINESIZE=	specifies linesize.
PAGESIZE=	specifies pagesize.
SPACES=	specifies number of spaces between output.
SPILL	specifies that a spill file be used.
CASE	specifies that the comparisons in data processing are case sensitive.
BREAK	enables a break exit and escape mechanism.

Table A3.9   Data Processing Commands

Opening and Closing

EDIT	opens a SAS data set for read and write access.
CREATE	opens a new SAS data set.
CLOSE	closes a SAS data set or external file.
SETIN	selects an open data set for input.
SETOUT	selects an open data set for output.
USE	opens a SAS data set for reading.

Showing and Resetting

SHOW DATASETS	shows data sets currently active.
SHOW CONTENTS	shows contents of current data set.
RESET DEFLIB=	sets up the default libname.
RESET CASE	does not convert comparison strings to uppercase.
RESET SPILL	allows spill file for large data sets.

Input and Output

LIST	displays records.
READ	reads data.
REPLACE	replaces data in a data set.
APPEND	adds records at the end of the data set.
FIND	finds records satisfying conditions.
DELETE	marks records as deleted.
FORCE	forces out data to a data set.
PURGE	purges deleted records from a SAS data set.

External Files

INFILE	opens to an external input file.
INPUT	reads from an external input file.
FILE	opens to an external output file.
PUT	writes to an external output file.
CLOSEFILE	closes an external file.

Applications

INDEX	indexes a data set.
SORT	sorts a data set.
SUMMARY	obtains summary statistics from a SAS data set.

(continued on next page)

Table A3.9   *(continued)*

Display Commands

WINDOW	opens a window on display.
DISPLAY	displays fields in a window.

Call Routines and Functions

DATASETS	is a function to obtain members in a data library.
CONTENTS	is a function to obtain variables in a member.
CALL RENAME	is a call routine to rename a SAS data set.
CALL DELETE	is a call routine to delete (erase) a SAS data set.

The MATRIX/IML™ Translator Procedure

ABSTRACT

The MATRIX/IML translator procedure translates PROC MATRIX code into PROC IML code. This translator is needed because MATRIX is being phased out and replaced by PROC IML.

INTRODUCTION

PROC MATRIX is a SAS procedure that implements a programming language that uses matrix algebra operators. PROC MATRIX works under IBM mainframe releases of SAS up through Version 5, but it is not included as part of Version 6.

Many PROC MATRIX users have programs that are hundreds, or in some cases thousands, of lines long. This procedure provides an aid to translating MATRIX code into IML code.

Although PROC MATRIX and PROC IML are similar, there are a number of incompatibilities that necessitate translating MATRIX code to be compatible with IML. In particular, the punctuation for subscripts and multi-element literal values is different. You should not regard the translation process as automatic. You still need to check the result.

Appendix 1 summarizes the differences between MATRIX and IML.

SPECIFICATIONS

The procedure is invoked as PROC MATIML. The only change you need to make to handle PROC MATRIX code is to change "PROC MATRIX" to "PROC MATIML" when you invoke the procedure:

PROC MATIML *options*;
    ...*matrix statements*...

DETAILS

Output

PROC MATIML writes the resulting translated code to the file assigned the fileref MATIML. Use the FILENAME statement prior to invoking PROC MATIML to make this assignment. If the fileref MATIML has not been assigned, the resulting code is written to the standard SAS print stream.

Translation Items

The following items are converted by the MATRIX/IML translator procedure. The nature of the translation is described.

subscripts
>   The PROC MATRIX "rule of first use" says that a name followed by a parenthesis connotes a subscript if the first use of the name has been as a variable not followed by parentheses. Otherwise, the construct is regarded as a function call. For subscripts, the parentheses are translated into square brackets.

numeric literals
>   MATRIX literals are a stream of numbers without braces or other enveloping punctuation. Where possible, minus signs are treated as signs on numbers rather than as minus operators. Slashes separate one row from the next. These MATRIX literals are translated to the IML convention that surrounds literals by braces and separates the rows with commas.

transpose quote mark
>   PROC MATIML translates a single quote into a backquote for the transpose operator unless the single quote is in a NOTE statement or at the start of an expression for a character literal assignment.

division
>   The MATRIX division operator #/ is translated to /.

LIST statement
>   The LIST statement is translated to

```
        SHOW NAMES SPACE;
```

NOTE statement
>   The NOTE statement is translated to a PRINT statement.

PRINT statement
>   During translation, the PRINT statement has commas inserted before each operand and brackets placed around the ROWNAME, COLNAME, and FORMAT options.

GO TO statement

The two-word GO TO statement is translated to a single word GOTO.

function calls

A dot between a name and an open-parenthesis (connoting a function call in MATRIX) is removed.

FETCH/OUTPUT statements

The FETCH statement is translated into USE/READ statements. The OUTPUT statement is translated into CREATE/APPEND or EDIT/APPEND statements. If several OUTPUT statements refer to the same data set, that is, if the OUT= value is textually identical on each of the statements, the first OUTPUT statement generates a CREATE/APPEND pair of PROC IML statements and all other OUTPUT statements referring to the data set produce EDIT/APPEND PROC IML statements.

The translator only supports the KEEP list data set option on FETCH statements. The KEEP list becomes the scope operand on the READ statement. If there is no KEEP list and no TYPE operand the scope of the READ command is VAR _ALL_. If TYPE=CHAR appears on the FETCH statement the scope operand is VAR _CHAR_. If the TYPE=NUM or TYPE=NUMERIC appears, the scope is VAR _NUM_. The translator flags other data set options as syntax errors. You should examine the translated results carefully and make adjustments as needed to the code.

SHAPE argument

An extra zero as a second argument is placed into invocations of the SHAPE function. This is necessary because the second argument for MATRIX is the number of columns, and for IML, it is the number of rows; the zero argument instructs IML to figure out the number of rows from the number of columns. This translation works even if you nest calls.

math commands

The SVD, EIGEN, and GS commands are translated into the corresponding call statements for IML.

comments

Comments in stream using /* and */ and statement comments starting the asterisk (*) and ending with semicolon are both copied into the output code.

upper/lowercase

The translator produces uppercase results, except for characters in quotes.

macros

Macros are not treated by the translator; they are processed by the normal SAS macro facility and then processed by the translator. You may have to hand edit the macro code before translating the MATRIX code with this procedure.

Cautions

The MATRIX/IML translator is not guaranteed to do a perfect conversion. You must check the result. The following items are not translated and must be converted by hand:

subscript reduction

> The dot (.) subscript reduction operator (for mean) is not correctly translated to a colon (:); it becomes a missing value literal instead. However, the following warning message is produced:

```
/* CHECK: period . may need to be colon if subscript */
```

> If you do not convert the dot to a semicolon, it results in execution errors for INDEXING, which can be readily diagnosed in the resulting program.

@|

> You must translate the horizontal direct product operator from MATRIX to an invocation of the HDIR function. The following warning message is produced to call attention to it:

```
/* CHECK: @| not converted, hand convert to HDIR */
```

EXAMPLE

Source Code	Resulting Code Stored in 'MATIML.OUT'

```
filename matiml 'matiml.out';      | PROC IML;
                                   | /*---start of MATRIX/IML translation---*/
proc matiml print fw=5 flow list;  | RESET PRINT FW=5 FLOW
                                   | /* CHECK: Feature LIST Not in Matrix */;
/*-literals-*/                     | /*-LITERALS-*/
a=1;                               | A={1};
b= 1 2 3 / 5 6 7;                  | B={ 1 2 3, 5 6 7};
c=-1 2;                            | C={-1 2};

/*-char literals and transpose-*/  | /*-CHAR LITERALS AND TRANSPOSE-*/
a='abc' 'def' 'geh';               | A=['abc' 'def' 'geh'];
b=a';      /* forward quote */     | B=A`;     /* FORWARD QUOTE */
c=b`;      /* backward quote */    | C=B`;     /* BACKWARD QUOTE */

/*-test functions vs. subscripts-*/| /*-TEST FUNCTIONS VS. SUBSCRIPTS-*/
b=a(1,2);      /* subscript*/      | B= A[{1},{2}]  /* SUBSCRIPT*/
c=sqrt(2);     /* function */      | C= SQRT({2});      /* FUNCTION */
d=a(1,2);      /* subscript*/      | D= A[{1},{2}] ;    /* SUBSCRIPT*/
e=a.(1,2);     /* function */      | E= A({1},{2});     /* FUNCTION */
r=sqrt.(2);    /* function */      | R= SQRT({2});   /* FUNCTION */
r=sqrt(a(1,2));                    | R= SQRT( A[{1},{2}]);
a(1,2)=a(sqrt(2),1);              | A[{1},{2}]= A[ SQRT({2}),{1}];
c=a(+,#);                          | C=[A +,#];

/*shape func. adds zero argument*/ | /*SHAPE FUNC. ADDS ZERO ARGUMENT*/
r=shape(a,2);                      | R= SHAPE(A,0,{2});

/*-if and do-*/                    | /*-IF AND DO-*/
if true=1 then                     | IF TRUE={1} THEN DO I={1} TO{5} WHILE(B);
```

```
do i=1 to 5 while(b);          |    H=I;
   h=i;                        |    END;
   end;                       | ELSE PRINT, A;
else print a;

do while(true);               |  DO WHILE(TRUE);
   do i=1 to 4 by -1;         |    DO I={1} TO{ 4} BY{-1};
      j=i;                     |      J=I;
      end;                     |      END;
   end;                        |    END;

/*-misc statements-*/         |  /*-MISC STATEMENTS-*/
note "here";                  |  PRINT "here";
list;                         |  SHOW SPACE NAMES;
goto 1;                       |  GOTO L;
go to 1;                      |  GOTO L;
print a rowname=r             |  PRINT, A[ ROWNAME=R]
        colname=c             |             [ COLNAME=C]
        format=f.;            |             [ FORMAT=F.] ;
svd a b c d;                  |  CALL SVD( A, B, C, D);
gs  a b c d;                  |  CALL GS(  A, B, C, D);
eigen a b c;                  |  CALL EIGEN( A, B, C);

/*-i/o statements-*/          |  /*-I/O STATEMENTS-*/
fetch a;                      |  USE _LAST_;
                              |  READ ALL INTO A ;
fetch a data=mem;             |  USE MEM;
                              |  READ ALL INTO A ;
fetch a rowname=r             |  USE LIB.MEM;
        data=lib.mem          |  READ ALL INTO A [ROWNAME=R]  [COLNAME=C] ;
        colname=c;

output a;                     |  CREATE _DATA_ FROM A;
                              |  APPEND FROM A;
output a out=mem;             |  CREATE MEM FROM A;
                              |  APPEND FROM A;
output a rowname=r            |  CREATE LIB.MEM FROM A[ROWNAME=R]
        out=lib.mem           |                       [COLNAME=C];
        colname=c;            |  APPEND FROM A[ROWNAME=R];

                              |  LABEL: PRINT "LABEL";
label: note label;            | /*---end of MATRIX/IML translation---*/
```

REFERENCES

SAS Institute Inc., "The Matrix Procedure: Language and Applications," *SAS Technical Report P-135,* Cary, NC, 1985.

SAS Institute Inc., *SAS User's Guide: Statistics, 1982 Edition,* Cary, NC, 1982.

References

Beaton, Albert (1964), "The Use of Special Matrix Operators in Statistical Calculus," *Research Bulletin*, Princeton: Educational Testing Service.

Cox, D.R. (1970), *The Analysis of Binary Data*, New York: Halsted Press.

Forsythe, G.E., Malcolm, M.A., and Moler, C.B. (1967), *Computer Solution of Linear Algebraic Systems*, Chapter 17, Englewood Cliffs, New Jersey: Prentice-Hall.

Goodnight, James H., (1979) "A Tutorial on the SWEEP Operator" *The American Statistician*, 33, 149-158.

Grizzle, J.E., Starmer, C.F., and Koch, G.G. (1969), "Analysis of Categorical Data by Linear Models," *Biometrics*, 25, 489-504.

Kaiser, H.F. and Caffrey, J. (1965), "Alpha Factor Analysis," *Psychometrika*, 30, 1-14.

Kastenbaum, M.A. and Lamphiear, D.E. (1959), "Calculation of Chi-Square to Test the No Three-Factor Interaction Hypothesis," *Biometrics*, 15, 107-122.

Kruskal, J.B. (1964), "Nonmetric Multidimensional Scaling," *Psychometrika*, 29, 1-27, 115-129.

Nobel, Ben (1969), *Applied Linear Algebra*, Englewood Cliffs, New Jersey: Prentice-Hall.

Pizer, Stephen M. (1975), *Numerical Computing and Mathematical Analysis*, Chicago: Science Research Associates, Inc.

Rao, C.R. and Mitra, Sujit Kumar (1971), *Generalized Inverse of Matrices and Its Applications*, New York: John Wiley & Sons.

Sall, John P. (1977), "Matrix Algebra Notation as a Computer Language," 1977 Statistical Computing Section of the American Statistical Association, Washington, D.C., 342-344.

Stanish, W. (1985), "Categorical Data Analysis Strategies Using SAS Software," *Computer Science and Statistics: Proceedings of the Seventeenth Symposium on the Interface*, Ed. by David M. Allen, Amsterdam: North-Holland.

Stoer, J. and Bulirsch, R. (1980), *Introduction to Numerical Analysis*, New York: Springer-Verlag.

Wilkinson, J.H. and Reinsch, C. (Editors), (1971), *Linear Algebra, Volume 2, Handbook for Automatic Computation*, New York: Springer-Verlag.

Young, F.W. (1981), "Quantitative Analysis of Qualitative Data," *Psychometrika*, 46, 357-388.

Index

Coding and proofing for this book were performed in the **Technical Writing Department** under the direction of **Gail C. Freeman** by coder **James K. Hart** and proofers **Frances A. Kienzle, E. Ellen Fussell, Mariam Chilman**, and **David A. Teal**.

Graphic Arts provided text composition and production under the direction of **Carol M. Thompson**. Text composition programmers were **Craig R. Sampson** and **Pamela A. Troutman**. For this book, **Arlene B. Drezek** and **Nancy K. Jones** were the compositors, and **Lisa N. Clements** was the artist.

Your Turn

If you have comments about SAS software or the *SAS/IML™Guide for Personal Computers, Version 6 Edition*, please send us your ideas on a photocopy of this page. If you include your name and address, we will reply to you.

Please return to the Publications Division, SAS Institute Inc., SAS Circle, Box 8000, Cary, NC 27511-8000.